THE MAN WITHIN

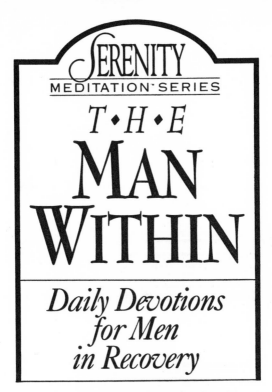

SERENITY
MEDITATION SERIES

T·H·E
MAN
WITHIN

*Daily Devotions
for Men
in Recovery*

Ted Scheuermann, Larry Stephens,
Brian Newman, and Bob Dyer

A
JANET
THOMA
BOOK

THOMAS NELSON PUBLISHERS
Nashville

Copyright © 1991 by Ted Scheuermann, Larry Stephens, Brian Newman, and Bob Dyer

Published in Nashville, Tennessee, by Thomas Nelson, Inc., and distributed in Canada by Lawson Falle, Ltd., Cambridge, Ontario.

Scripture quotations are from the NEW KING JAMES VERSION of the Bible. Copyright © 1979, 1980, 1982, Thomas Nelson, Inc., Publishers.

Scripture quotations marked NIV are taken from The Holy Bible: NEW INTERNATIONAL VERSION. Copyright © 1978 by the New York International Bible Society. Used by permission of Zondervan Bible Publishers.

Library of Congress Cataloging-in-Publication Data

The Man within / Ted Scheuermann . . . [et al.].
     p.   cm. — (Serenity meditation series)
  "A Janet Thoma book."
  ISBN 0-8407-3240-6 (pbk.)
  1. Twelve-step programs—Religious aspects—Meditations. 2. Devotional calendars.
I. Scheuermann, Ted. II. Series.
BL624.5.M36 1991
242'.4—dc20   91–28448
                       CIP

Printed in the United States of America
1 2 3 4 5 6 7 — 96 95 94 93 92 91

*The Twelve Steps of Alcoholics Anonymous**

1. We admitted we were powerless over alcohol—that our lives had become unmanageable. 2. Came to believe that a Power greater than ourselves could restore us to sanity. 3. Made a decision to turn our will and our lives over to the care of God as we understood Him. 4. Made a searching and fearless moral inventory of ourselves. 5. Admitted to God, to ourselves, and to another human being the exact nature of our wrongs. 6. Were entirely ready to have God remove all these defects of character. 7. Humbly asked Him to remove our shortcomings. 8. Made a list of all persons we had harmed and became willing to make amends to them all. 9. Made direct amends to such people wherever possible, except when to do so would injure them or others. 10. Continued to take personal inventory and when we were wrong, promptly admitted it. 11. Sought through prayer and meditation to improve our conscious contact with God, as we understood Him, praying only for knowledge of His will for us and the power to carry that out. 12. Having had a spiritual awakening as the result of these steps, we tried to carry this message to alcoholics and to practice these principles in all our affairs.

*The Twelve Steps are reprinted and adapted with permission of Alcoholics Anonymous World Services, Inc. Permission to reprint and adapt Twelve Steps does not mean that AA has reviewed or approved the content of this publication, nor that AA agrees with the views expressed herein. AA is a program of recovery from alcoholism. Use of the Twelve Steps in connection with programs and activities which are patterned after AA but which address other problems does not imply otherwise. The Twelve Steps are referred to and quoted individually throughout the book.

Introduction

Sometimes what men need most is another man to talk with, another man who will share their burden as they walk the path of recovery. Recovery doesn't happen overnight. It is a one step at a time, one day at a time process. It starts with realizing that you must rely not on your own strength but on God's power. And you keep going with the help and support of friends with whom you are willing to struggle and be honest.

As we have counseled others or been counseled ourselves, each of us has confronted issues of recovery—the need to admit our shortcomings, the need to have help and support, fears of inadequacy and the loss of a personal sense of worth and value, the temptations to take a break from recovery. The process can seem overwhelming. But through the grace and love of God and the Twelve Steps of Alcoholics Anonymous, which has helped hundreds of thousands of men and women in recovery from abuse and addictions, those we have counseled have found the help they need to overcome their shortcomings and gain peace of mind and spirit and freedom in relationships with others. We want you to know this same grace and love.

In *The Man Within*, we have told stories from our personal and clinical experiences. A recovering alcoholic with twelve years of sobriety, Ted Scheuermann is program coordinator of the MAN-TO-MAN program, sponsored by the Christian Service Brigade. Larry Stephens is a licensed professional counselor and a certified alcohol and drug abuse counselor in the state of Texas. He counsels groups and individuals on an inpatient and outpatient basis with the Minirth-Meier Clinic in Dallas. Bob Dyer, a licensed minister, is the director of Seminars and Information Services at the Minirth-Meier Clinic in Dallas, Texas. And with his D.Phil., Brian Newman is clinical director of Inpatient Services at the Minirth-Meier Clinic in Dallas. We have identified the devotionals we have written by placing our initials in the lower corner of each devotional.

You can follow the Twelve Steps of Alcoholics Anonymous throughout the year. The stories we recount are true—stories of men's abusive behavior toward others, honest confrontations with homosexuality, and addictions to alcohol and other chemical substances, work, food, sex, rage—though we have disguised the personalities of those we have met in our offices and changed the details of their lives to protect their privacy.

We wish you God's grace and health.

Ted, Larry, Brian, and Bob

*We admitted we were powerless over alcohol—that
our lives had become unmanageable.*
—THE TWELVE STEPS OF ALCOHOLICS ANONYMOUS*

*Therefore I take pleasure in infirmities, in
reproaches, in needs, in persecutions, in
distresses, for Christ's sake. For when I
am weak, then I am strong.* —2 COR. 12:10

For thirty-three years I made it on my own. I didn't
need anyone. I could do it. But on January 17, 1979, I
couldn't do it any more. I was beat. I was finished. I
thought the game of life was over because I was weak.

Twelve years later, I know the truth. I wasn't strong
during those early years; I was in bondage to myself,
my wants, and my desires and to alcohol. My true
strength began with my defeat, my admission of powerlessness in 1979. Since that time, I truly am strong.
I'm strong in the dependence upon Jesus Christ that
makes me so. I'm strong when I realize my powerlessness, my need to have the Lord run my life. Like Paul,
"when I am weak, then I am strong."

*Lord, make me aware again of my powerlessness over people,
places, and things. Help me to claim the strength that You have provided for me.*

T. S.

---

*The Twelve Steps are printed in full on page *v* and are quoted throughout
the book!

> *Let us search out and examine our ways,*
> *And turn back to the LORD.*
>
> —LAM. 3:40

Some of the most common phrases I run across when dealing with men who have addictions are: "I can stop anytime I want to"; "I've gone months without using or abusing"; and "If I can just quit doing this, I'll be all right." These beliefs only serve to hinder the man who wishes to be in recovery. Recovery is much more than mere abstinence. Abstinence only puts the addiction cycle in a state of remission and stops the vicious cycle. As I have told patients over and over, "Anyone can stop his addiction temporarily." But it is the element of pride that comes with believing that one has control over his addiction that precedes the fall.

Abstinence is only the first step of recovery. Recovery is a lifelong, dynamic growth encounter. It involves a complete mental, emotional, spiritual, and physical overhaul; numerous lifestyle and personality changes; and a discovery of the underlying problems that drive the addiction.

Therefore be thankful for the time in which you are not acting out your addiction; but be sure at the same time that you are committed to the deeper work of recovery.

Lord, help me to understand the true motives of my behavior.

L. S.

*But whoever has this world's goods, and sees his
brother in need, and shuts up his heart from him,
how does the love of God abide in him?*
—1 JOHN 3:17

An epidemic is spreading throughout Christianity. Its potential is enormous, and it has already hurt untold numbers. We limit Christ's abundance and the bread of life to spiritual concerns. Many are starving physically, but we refuse to meet those needs. This is a question of obedience, not to mention the heart. Is our culture so infecting Christianity that we only look out for number one?

As we have grown through heartache and life's valleys, should we not offer help to those still in pain? One of the greatest things a person can do for another is help to feed him. Whether with food or compassion, we must give of ourselves. How can we speak of the love of Christ and not exemplify it? If you have come from a period of darkness and know of someone else's pain, what better time than the present to share with another? The benefits are just as great for you. When we take the care to help someone and see the positive result, we can't help but feel good for him as well as ourselves. An even greater benefit is knowing that God is pleased.

Father, I pray that I see need in others and fill it, see thirst in others and quench it, see hunger in others and stop it.

B. D.

> *And you He made alive, who were dead in trespasses and sins, in which you once walked according to the course of this world, according to the prince of the power of the air, the spirit who now works in the sons of disobedience.*
>
> —EPH. 2:1–2

I woke up—came to, really—at about three o'clock Sunday morning. I was in great pain. Sprawled half on my unmade bed, half on the floor, blood everywhere, face down in my own vomit, I tried to remember what happened. I was in desperate shape. *I might as well be dead,* I thought.

Three months later alcoholism brought me to my knees. Spiritually, emotionally, I was dead—"dead in trespasses and sins, a son of disobedience."

In a treatment center, Jesus made me alive to the truth of His gospel, filled with love for and from others whom He has also made alive.

Some of you who read this know life this way . . . by having been made alive after you were already dead. Praise God with me today for the love He sent our way in Jesus Christ.

Almighty God, thank You for finding us dead in sin, for loving us that way, for sending Jesus to make us alive again. Thank You, Jesus, for my life.

T. S.

*Be anxious for nothing, but in everything by prayer
and supplication, with thanksgiving, let your
requests be made known to God.*   —PHIL. 4:6

The addictive personality does not know how or when
to say no. The male addict wants what he wants, right
now, yesterday. If he does not get what he wants immediately, he will make everyone around as miserable as
he believes he is. If this doesn't work, he may turn to
manipulation, anger, seduction, or rage. If he is still un-
successful, he may turn to more passive tactics such as
pouting, noncompliance, or sarcasm. Eventually this
man will get what he wants, no matter what the cost.

These self-serving behaviors originate in infancy. An
infant is egocentric and self-serving. Babies are unable
to think about others when they want something; they
just want it. Addictive personalities function at this in-
fantile level.

Recovery involves growth in the ability to delay
gratification. In recovery the addictive man realizes
that he is not the only one in the world. He learns to
consider the feelings and needs of others, to give
rather than always receive. As a man surrenders his
will to God, energy that was once wasted in the service
of constant pleasure seeking is now available to be
channeled into positive and more productive behaviors.

Lord, help me to want for nothing.

L. S.

> *[Barnabas] encouraged them all that with purpose*
> *of heart they should continue with the Lord. For he*
> *was a good man, full of the Holy Spirit and*
> *of faith.*
> —ACTS 11:23–24

John had been struggling in his marriage and felt like he couldn't play the game anymore. He left his wife and two children. Chris heard what John had done. Although he lived six hundred miles away, he took a weekend to drive out to see John. Chris knew that what John needed was not judgment, but encouragement. Chris shared his concern, love, and support. Through talking and prayer he was able to encourage John to go back to his family.

What so many men lack is another man who will look them eye to eye and offer a strong shoulder of support. That support may come in different ways. Sometimes it is through love and caring; other times, through confrontation and accountability. Lives are changed when men are willing to reach beyond themselves and their own concerns and get involved in other men's lives.

Man-to-man encouragement has a different kind of power than woman-to-man. A man can relate to the struggles of another man. Men need other men who will get involved with them in a strong way. Are you willing to be that kind of man?

Lord, help me be open and aware of hurting men around me, and give me strength to encourage them.

B. N.

For the good that I will to do, I do not do; but the evil I will not to do, that I practice.

—ROM. 7:19

It's easy to believe that we are powerless: airplane crashes, traffic accidents, cancer. Sure, I can say I'm powerless over alcohol, drugs, sexual addiction, overwork. I know I need God's help to keep me away from these things that enslave me, that will kill me if they get a foothold.

Lurking in the shadows, pleased to hear me think this way, is that ultimate bondage of *self!* "But he had such good intentions," we hear our friends say. "How could he have gone so wrong?"

How, indeed? Left to my own devices, allowing myself to have my own good ideas, I am set up for a fall. On my own, with all my good intentions, I will do what I do not want to do and neglect what I should be doing.

God is the key to this mystery, the answer for me. My life, left to me, is utterly unmanageable. I need His help. His Word and the people He's put in my life, who love me with His tough love, can help me find and stay on the right track.

Lord, remind me today that You, not I, are the boss.

T. S.

See that no one renders evil for evil to anyone, but always pursue what is good both for yourselves and for all.

—1 THESS. 5:15

Have you ever asked anyone to play a game, a sport or a board game, without having the covert goal to win, and without having some kind of secret game strategy? Have you ever been excited or happy when someone finally agreed to play with you? If you answered yes to either question, then you are probably familiar with the art of game playing.

People play covert games with us to reaffirm their view of who they are and who they think we are. There are basically four types of games: "I'm okay— you're okay"; "I'm okay—you're not okay"; "I'm not okay—you're okay"; and "I'm not okay—you're not okay." For example, if your boss criticizes you constantly, he is probably trying to get you to feel that you're not okay and to help himself feel that he is okay. If he succeeds in making you feel bad inside, then he wins the game.

People try to get me to play these games for their own good at my expense. I used to play these games, but now I realize that I don't have to. I only place myself in relationships where both parties can come out okay.

People who hurt you are almost always hurt themselves; they just want you to feel as bad as they do.

L. S.

Again, the kingdom of heaven is like a merchant seeking beautiful pearls, who, when he had found one pearl of great price, went and sold all that he had and bought it. —MATT. 13:45–46

Often men and women in recovery struggle with a loss of personal worth and value. Their sense of value has been diminished. I spoke with a man who for years had been successful in his business. For several months his business suffered severely. The more his business dwindled, the easier it became for him to see himself as a failure, unloved, and of no value. As we spoke, he realized that his self-concept was based on achievement and others' approval.

Goals and the approval and appreciation of others are good. Finding our value solely in them, though, is dangerous. Self-worth that depends on achievement or jobs or even people is flimsy at best. Self-worth and value found in a relationship with the Father is unchanging.

The merchant in the verse above is God, and the pearl is you. When He found you He sold His only son Jesus Christ. That is the value God the Father places on you. Here we find our worth.

Father, may I never forget the price You paid for me and the value You placed on my soul.

B. D.

> *And a great windstorm arose, and the waves beat
> into the boat, so that it was already filling. . . . And
> they awoke Him and said to Him, "Teacher, do You
> not care that we are perishing?"*
>
> MARK 4:37–38

There are no atheists in foxholes." We've all heard that many times. Unfortunately, it's all too true. We all seem to be able to put our mortality out of our minds. Most addicts have developed this ability into an art. "Let's not think about that today," we say. "We'll think about that *tomorrow*." But when the reality of our own tenuous existence comes crashing down on us like the waves of the sea on that little boat, we suddenly realize we must work on it today . . . *RIGHT NOW!*

For me, for all of us "addicts," real change comes only when we are willing to surrender completely, to say "I am powerless," to realize that the boat will begin to ship water the minute we try to sail it alone. We need to wake the Lord up, admit that we cannot handle the boat, and let Him take over.

Lord, let me remember the moment when I woke You up. Help me today to be a willing deckhand on the boat of my life.

T. S.

*You shall not lie with a male as with a woman. It is
an abomination.* —LEV. 18:22

As Brad anxiously sat in my office he began to tell
me of his struggle with homosexuality. He had been
involved sexually with men since he was a teenager.
Brad felt powerless over the homosexual impulses at
times.

What was the prescription for Brad? Not a sermon or
spiritual condemnation. Yes, it is true that both the Old
Testament and New Testament categorically condemn
homosexuality. But Brad was searching for an external
experience to fill an empty love. And he was caught in
a vicious shame cycle, driven by his own social and
emotional isolation.

Brad's recovery first involved his realizing that his
sexual feelings for other men were not wrong in themselves. Almost all men have some latent homosexual
desires. Second, Brad had to realize that lusting and
acting on these feelings *were* wrong. Third, Brad had
to realize that his addiction to this external experience
would never meet his true needs. Fourth, he had to
realize that he had confused sex with intimacy and
nurture. Finally, Brad had to work a Twelve Step program to control these compulsions and to learn healthy
ways to find intimacy.

Lord, teach me healthy ways to meet my intimacy needs.

L. S.

For God so loved the world that He gave His only begotten Son.
—JOHN 3:16

Christopher Leach's *Letter to a Younger Son* describes the events and his feelings after the unexpected death of his elder son. I'll never forget the words on the inside cover of the book: "This book leads to a series of reflections by a man who, poleaxed by the tragedy, and without the support of religious belief, attempts to find an answer that will allow him to live with the unacceptable."

I recall vividly the day my father passed away. I can't imagine the pain of losing my son. Yes, I believe I would have a hard time accepting it too. I assume Mr. Leach cried out in grief as would I. But here the similarities end. Whereas Mr. Leach came to a conclusion about his son's death, I believe he never found true empathy in his friends or his philosophies.

As tragedy strikes, it is of unequivocal value to know that our God knows the pain of lost love. His comfort is cloaked in the Holy Spirit and conveyed in His Word. Never shall we wonder if anyone knows our pain. The God of the universe, the God of Salvation, the Father of Christ Jesus our Lord knows all too well.

Lord, in You I find comfort, and in You I will again experience joy.
B. D.

*While they promise them liberty, they themselves
are slaves of corruption; for by whom a person is
overcome, by him also he is brought into bondage.*
—2 PETER 2:19

*A*lcoholics Anonymous mentions the "bondage of
self." I was overcome with self. To use Twelve-step lan-
guage, I was like a "prideful balloon" seeking to float
above the heads of my "lesser" brothers. And my preoccupation with my own dear self caused me to be in
bondage . . . to myself.

When I felt bad, I needed to find something to make
me feel good—never mind what God wanted for me. If
I wanted something, I had to have it—never mind what
the Lord thought about it. If I hated someone, that was
reason enough to hurt him—never mind Jesus and the
Sermon on the Mount.

The inevitable result? Emotionally, spiritually, I died.
But the Hound of Heaven never gave up. One day,
when I was totally alone and broken, God put me in
touch with people who were free. They worshiped
Him from glad, sincere, and grateful hearts. Slowly,
often painfully, I, too, was freed by Jesus to be free
indeed.

*Lord Jesus, help me to celebrate my freedom today by leading me to
someone who is in bondage as I once was, and let me share Your
good news with them.*

T. S.

Grace to you and peace be multiplied.
—1 PETER 1:2

Many men cherish having nothing to do. This is not true for men who have compulsive personalities. For them occupied time is of the essence—they must be busy.

For the compulsive male, time which is unfilled equals boredom and therefore guilt or depression. The male who believes that he must stay busy feels guilty if he wastes time. He also feels depressed because he only feels worthwhile if he is doing.

Staying busy and abusing chemicals serve as anesthetics that numb the compulsive male's pain. They also reinforce his craving for stimulation.

A compulsive type of personality must tell himself that it is all right to read or do nothing at times. Although it will take your feelings a while to catch up with your mind, continue to correct the lie that you must stay busy. Practice spending specific periods of time doing nothing. For example, just sit in a chair for one hour and allow yourself to enjoy the feeling of relaxation. The key to freedom is balance and control. Remember that Jesus lived a balanced life. He knew when to eat, sleep, work, and pray.

Lord, help me learn to appreciate my quiet moments.

L. S.

We were well pleased to impart to you not only the gospel of God, but also our own lives.
—1 THESS. 2:8

Men need other men who will look them straight in the eye and open up their hearts and souls. Paul didn't just share a message—the gospel—but he also shared his life. Men are not always comfortable sharing their lives. Often they don't understand what it is to share their hearts and souls.

A man I met on an airplane had all the distinctions of a successful businessman. He seemed to have it all. Although we were total strangers, he shared about his life, his struggles with his teenage son, and how he longed to find a way to help his wife forgive him for his past unfaithfulness.

Many men are involved in this man's life, looking to him as the kind of man they want to be. Few men would feel they had much to offer him. I shared parts of my life with him, and when the plane landed, out walked not a successful businessman and a counselor, but two men who had been encouraged by sharing deeply about their lives—not sharing answers but sharing struggles.

Christ gave His life. All He asks is that we men share our lives with others.

Lord, help me today to be real with friends and to give them the best part of my life.

B. N.

> *Have mercy on me, O LORD, for I am weak;*
> *O LORD, heal me, for my bones are troubled.*
> —PS. 6:2

Ivan recently had surgery for throat cancer. The treatment was so extreme that he almost died. And while he was sick, I discovered how important he has been to my recovery. Oh, I still don't know many of the facts of his life, but he has given me a gift through our twelve years of sharing together at meetings.

He always introduces himself this way: "My name is Ivan and I'm an alcoholic, sober today by God's grace through the fellowship of Alcoholics Anonymous." He's been sober over twenty years and knows a lot about God's grace. He depends on God for his sobriety.

"I was going to hell on a sled, more dead than alive," he says, "when one morning I decided I had had enough. I called AA that day, and nothing has been the same since. God, through His grace, keeps me sober one day at a time."

Something about Ivan's little statement reminds me of the troubled bones that David talked about. And Ivan's simple dependence and assurance are his gift to me.

Lord Jesus, help me to appreciate the incredible grace You provide for me today.

T. S.

*I know whom I have believed and am persuaded
that He is able to keep what I have committed to
Him until that Day.* —2 TIM. 1:12

Remember when you were a little boy and you used
to watch the escalator going up and down while your
parents were shopping? If you were like me, you had to
try to climb up the down escalator. I personally remembered thinking that the climb would be fun and
easy, but it was exhausting and scary instead. During
one climb in a department store, I had made it almost
to the top and stopped for a second to rest. I felt that I
had plenty of time before reaching the bottom to climb
back up, but I panicked as I realized that I wasn't going
to have the strength to complete the climb. On the way
down I just knew that I was going to be swallowed up
by the teeth of this monster.

This story illustrates the process of recovery. In
many ways recovery is like going up a down escalator.
The escalator of addiction, though, is seemingly eternal; it never stops moving. Ever so slowly it continues
to move, defying the strength of any man trying to
make the recovery climb.

The climb does get easier as you grow in the
strength of your recovery, but every time you take a
break from your recovery program, you are going
backward a few feet. Before you decide to get off the
recovery track, make sure you can afford it.

Lord, give me the strength and patience to make the recovery climb.

L. S.

> *. . . knowing that tribulation produces*
> *perseverance; and perseverance, character;*
> *and character, hope.*
> —ROM. 5:3b–4

Tim believed he could go no further. The road had been so long and it didn't seem to get any easier. Yet he could see progress. Two long years had passed since his world came crashing down. A loving family came apart and a career ended.

Our lives do change. It is not always easy or enjoyable. The outcome isn't always our desire. But our lives can and do change.

From the thirst of the alcoholic to the pangs of the overeater, we must know there is hope. Hope moves us down the track fueled by perseverance, the motivation that says, "I've come this far, I will take another step."

Steps are taken one after another. After we've taken several we can look back and judge our progress. Fatigue and frustration may set in but even when we stumble, we rise to our feet and take another step forward.

Tim's life was changing, slowly, sometimes painfully, progressing—by perseverance, toward hope.

Lord, even in times of darkness You are my light.

B. D.

*But when he came to himself, he said, ". . . my
father's hired servants have bread enough and to
spare, and I perish with hunger! I will arise and go
to my father. . . ."*
                                    —LUKE 15:17–18

Maybe you have heard the old truism, "When you
find yourself far from God, who moved?" When we feel
alienated from God, when something is not right between Him and us, who is to blame?

I think we are. My friend Mary says we are problem
people. Difficulties seem to surround me much of the
time, and God is not to blame—I am. Like the prodigal,
unfortunately, I have periods of time when I "perish
with hunger" for God. Perhaps I need such times to
fully appreciate His provision for all my needs, but I
suspect it has more to with relearning the first step—
that I am powerless and lead an unmanageable life if I
do not let God take control.

How is it with you and the first step today? Are you
"biting off more than you can chew"? Do you need to
"let go and let God" today?

---

*Dear God, remind me today of my total inability to handle anything
without Your help. Help me to let You manage what I cannot control.*
                                                        T. S.

> *Be careful to do as the LORD your God has*
> *commanded you; you shall not turn aside*
> *to the right hand or to the left.* —DEUT. 5:32

Almost every day some noted individual is brought up for fraud or tax evasion. The motto at the top must be "The higher I go, the more corners I'll cut." But men who cut corners at the top probably started cutting corners at the bottom. In fact, that may have been how they made it to the top.

Maybe you are not well known, but perhaps you have been involved in some not quite ethical activities in your own job or business: not reporting taxes, bending tax rules, cheating on expense reports, breaking company rules and not following policies, making exceptions, using the company car for personal use, or even embezzling money.

Men are encouraged to get rich and to be highly successful; this is society's prescription for happiness. To fill this prescription quickly, many men break the rules. Some men actually believe that they are entitled to be above the rules and that the company owes them more than a salary. Others are told by their supervisors to break the rules or lose their jobs.

As Christians we are to be beyond reproach in our business and personal dealings. It is better to climb to the top honestly than to cut yourself into a hole too deep to climb out of.

You come into this world with nothing, and man owes you nothing.

L. S.

He who guards his mouth preserves his life,
But he who opens wide his lips shall have
destruction. —PROV. 13:3

Confidentiality in support groups is very important. It is hard for some people to keep something secret or confidential. For some, the thrill of knowing a secret is telling it to someone else. God warns us that sharing too much can get us into trouble.

Ben's experience illustrates this. He came to counseling to deal with his anger and despair over a situation that happened to him. His wife left him, and his children were taken away from him because she accused him of sexually abusing the children. Ben was innocent and was proven so by the court. By then, however, a lot of damage had been done to his reputation, and his relationship with his children was affected. Word about Ben's situation was quick to spread around the town and to his friends. Many people didn't know if they could truly trust him after all the accusations.

It's important to think about the information we give to others. Are there some things we say about other people that are better left unsaid?

God, help me to choose my words wisely and honestly.

B. N.

> *How long, O LORD? Will You forget me forever?*
> *How long will You hide Your face from me?*
> —PS. 13:1

Have you reached bottom yet? Are you ready to quit? Does it seem that God has forgotten you forever? If so, that's good!

No, I'm not a sadist . . . and neither is God! But I have learned that when we quit, we win. That's right; there's strength in weakness, wholeness in personal destruction, fellowship in isolation, and security in fear. Each and every negative feeling contains the seeds of recovery. So if God seems far away today, take time to reestablish contact.

He wants to hear from you. Why? Because He loves you and wants your fellowship. So, right now, give God all the pain, heartache, fear, and suffering you have. Let Him replace it with security, strength, fellowship, and wholeness.

Dear Lord, I surrender all I have tried to carry alone to You today. Please replace it all with the peace that passes understanding that You promise.

T. S.

*For God has not given us a spirit of fear, but
of power and of love and of a sound mind.*
—2 TIM. 1:7

One of the most fearful years that I can remember was my seventh-grade year. That year two bullies marked me as a victim, probably because I was under-developed both physically and emotionally.

During the year these two bullies were after me, I was terrified to go to gym class, terrified to walk the halls, and paralyzed at the sound of the last school bell. Every opportunity they had, they hit me or mocked me; I just hated it.

When I talked with my dad about the problem, he told me that I had to stand up to them. I reluctantly did it. I was terrified as I broke James' nose and cracked a clipboard over Chuck's head. As you may already have expected, I was beaten up that day in the worst way. But neither of them ever bothered me again.

A fear is like a bully. It waits for you at every corner. It terrifies and immobilizes you. It will not go away on its own and will never leave you alone unless you confront it. In the process of facing your fear you may be hurt or injured, but freedom will be worth the pain.

Remember that if you don't face your fears, they will have power over you.

L. S.

> *And there is no creature hidden from His sight, but all things are naked and open to the eyes of Him to whom we must give account.* —HEB. 4:13

Many men who consider themselves pretty honest guys don't realize how much they deceive themselves. Usually they are so busy covering up their weakness that they don't realize how afraid they are of being seen as weak.

Although we may try to play a game before God, too, He knows we are weak. He loves and accepts us in spite of our weaknesses.

George told me he had cheated on his income tax. He proudly rationalized that the IRS had so much money they would never miss the couple of hundred bucks he didn't pay. But George felt like a failure before God. The real reason George had cheated on the taxes was that he couldn't face his wife with the truth that he couldn't buy her the diamond earrings he promised. He ended up deceiving his wife and himself, but he couldn't deceive God. When he told the truth to God, himself and his wife, his wife made him as miserable as he feared she would. But an honest relationship with God and himself was worth it.

God, help me to live today in honesty and courage.

B. N.

*Their sorrows shall be multiplied who hasten
after another god.* —PS. 16:4

When I was a young boy in Sunday school, I first heard of the Ten Commandments. Besides not knowing what some of the words meant, I kept track of which sins I thought I had committed or not committed. When someone told me that *covet* meant to want something that belonged to someone else, I knew I did that one. And when "bear false witness" was explained to me, I knew I was in big trouble. But I thought for many years that I was safe when it came to idolatry. How wrong I was!

My dictionary defines *idolatry* as blind and obsessive admiration for a person or a thing. I had an obsession for myself and for alcohol. In fact, I cannot tell you where bondage to myself left off and bondage to alcohol began. They were inseparable. It was very important that I "feel good" regardless of the cost. I was a slave to my feelings.

Heavenly Father, please protect me from the bondage of self. It is my desire to worship only You, not myself or my feelings.

T. S.

> *Do not let your heart turn aside*
> *to her ways,*
> *Do not stray into her paths.*
> —PROV. 7:25

Voyeurism is the act of looking at a woman for sexual gratification. It is not limited to peeping into windows. Many of us have been voyeurs. After all, men applaud inconspicuous girl watching.

Mark's obsession was girl watching. Everywhere he went, he was undressing the girls who walked by in his mind. This was soon not enough. He began secretly taking photographs of women. Even this was not enough, so Mark started frequenting strip joints. By the time Mark saw me for counseling, he had lost his wife, who had found his secret photographs, and his job because of absenteeism. Mark was depressed and defeated. He couldn't understand how things became so out of control.

Mark's control was lost early when he started taking the photographs. At this point he crossed the invisible line into addiction. He only had an illusion of control. Powerless, he was no longer deciding when he would act out; the addiction was.

Who's in control of your sexual behavior? Check to see if it's really you.

God, help me to turn my eyes upward to You instead of down.

L. S.

*For he who doubts is like a wave of the sea driven
and tossed by the wind.* —JAMES 1:6b

Growing up in Houston, Texas, brings an appreciation of severe weather, especially during hurricane season. As a teenager I had a friend whose family owned a boat that they kept anchored down on the Gulf Coast. One season a hurricane was developing, and everyone was taking precautions in Galveston and in the bays. There was no time for my friend and his family to check on their boat. They just had to trust that they had secured and anchored it well.

The storm came through and did considerable damage. I was asked to join my friend when he went to assess the damage to his boat. We saw boats tossed and mangled like so much litter, but to our surprise and joy my friend's boat had weathered the storm. By securing the boat effectively and firmly anchoring it, he had averted disaster.

Our lives are like that boat. Life's storms rock us and toss us about, but we have a safe harbor and refuge in Christ and in God's Word.

God is not only our anchor in rough times; He also calms the seas.

Father, You are my refuge and safety. Remind me of Your protection.

B. D.

> *Came to believe that a Power greater than ourselves*
> *could restore us to sanity.*
> —THE TWELVE STEPS OF ALCOHOLICS ANONYMOUS

> *Let Your mercy, O Lord, be upon us,*
> *Just as we hope in You.*
> —PS. 33:22

According to the preamble of AA, it is a "fellowship of men and women who share their experience, strength and hope with each other that they may solve their common problem and help others to recover from alcoholism." Why is hope so important?

Many, if not most of us, come to Twelve Step programs as a last resort; those with eating disorders, for example, have tried every diet imaginable. Alcoholics have tried and failed again and again to stop drinking. Compulsive gamblers have lost all they had. We are morally and spiritually bankrupt.

How important, then, that we be given hope from those around us. As Twelve-Step people share their hope in "God as they understand Him," we begin to hope in Him as well. As we hope in Him, He is merciful to us. How often people new to the Twelve Steps are amazed by merciful, grace-filled acceptance. God truly showers mercy upon us as we hope in Him.

Dear God, thank You for the promise of Your mercy as we hope in You. I reiterate my hope in You today and claim Your mercy.

T. S.

*Count it all joy when you fall into various trials,
knowing that the testing of your faith produces
patience.*
                                    —JAMES 1:2–3

If you were to imagine the worst two things that were to happen to you, one of them would probably be the loss of a job. Unemployment has to be one of the most difficult valleys a man can walk through. The effects of being laid off or fired run right to the heart of a man's identity, pride, and self-worth. When I once was unable to find work, I felt more depressed and worthless than I ever had before. I felt guilty for not providing for my wife and useless around the house. My manhood was further threatened as I was turned down by employer after employer.

I was much harder on myself than I needed to be. One of the reasons I felt so worthless is that I based my self-worth in my work. I also entertained some false guilt. It was not my fault that I was out of work, and I continued to look for work daily even though I was depressed. Finally, I must not have trusted God a lot back then. That's why I did so much worrying. In fact, I distinctly remember being angry at God.

If you are unemployed and are waiting to enter the work force again, do not add injury to your self-worth by condemning yourself, and do not feed your own guilt unless you're not trying. God has not abandoned you.

Lord, help me to preserve life without work, one day at a time.

                                                    L. S.

I sought the LORD, and He heard me,
And delivered me from all my fears.
—PS. 34:4

The world is unstable. There are many reasons for a person—even a man—to be afraid. There is the rise in crime, war, earthquakes, etc. Men have a hard time acknowledging and expressing their fears. Many men are brought up to believe that it is "sissy" to be scared.

When I finished my graduate training in counseling, I started a new job. My wife and I had been married for only a short time. The job was very slow in getting started, and I was working on commission. I remember struggling with a lot of fears. Was I going to be able to provide for my new bride? Was I going to have to go into a lot of financial debt? Maybe you've had fears like these.

All men have fears, and we can find comfort from God about those fears if we will look to Him. God can and wants to give you peace and relief from your fears. First, admit they are there, and then pray about them to Him. There is nothing unmasculine about that.

God, help me to seek You today and to turn my fears over to You.

B. N.

He also brought me out into a broad place;
He delivered me because He delighted in me.
—PS. 18:19

The second step comes alive for me through the examples of others. Mary is such an example to me. She grew up in an alcoholic family (her father and all of her brothers and sisters are alcoholic) and was widowed in her mid-thirties with four small children. Naturally, she turned to alcohol for relief. After several years, she reached AA, where I met her.

When we first met, I was very sick. Mary was in her mid-forties then, good-looking and pleasant, a great listener. I couldn't imagine that she had ever been as sick as I was then. Still, her words rang true. As this healthy woman related her story to me, she served as an example of the second step. I could have faith that there was a God who could restore me to sanity. Mary was proof of that.

God, thank You for providing examples like Mary for me, to show me what You can do with someone like me. Help me, too, to be an example to others.

T. S.

> *Let this mind be in you which was also in*
> *Christ Jesus.*
>
> PHIL. 2:5

Why do we fantasize so much, led by illusive dreams of more erotic and more fulfilling sexual encounters? Partly out of our own perceptions of sexual depravity, partly out of the psychology of more. Out of our own deep inferiority and shame, we are driven towards illusive encounters with the women of our dreams or, as some psychologists would say, our fantasy moms. We somehow believe that if only our sexual fantasies could come true, then our deep void would finally be filled.

This illusion is utterly false. If there were actually some legitimacy in sexual fantasy, it would be only in its ability to sustain sexual satisfaction between two married partners. Men I have counseled have been severely let down after acting out their fantasies. They also were ashamed afterward. They could have been saved the pain if they had known that fantasy is only exciting if it remains fantasy. And they could have avoided the shame had they known that the only healthy and legitimately satisfying fantasy is one about their wives.

———————

God, help me to live in reality and to dream only of my wife.

L. S.

By pride comes only contention,
But with the well-advised is wisdom.
—PROV. 13:10

Men are considered the prideful sex. How many times have you or other men you have known wasted gallons of gas trying to reach a new destination without admitting you're lost? One of the passengers may suggest that you stop and ask for directions, but this only increases your determination to find the location on your own.

Men who struggle with pride are afraid of showing that they are weak, vulnerable, or inadequate. They fear their imperfections. Proverbs warns us that pride brings strife but wisdom comes from being well advised. Men need to understand the need to support and to learn from one another. If we are having problems with our family or in business, we must seek help from other men whom we can trust to give us wise counsel.

When I had automobile trouble, I was told to wait a while before correcting the problem. I didn't listen, and in my haste I ended up causing more damage. It was an expensive lesson.

Lord, give me wisdom to see my pride and to turn to wise counsel for help.

B. N.

> *Some trust in chariots, and some in horses;*
> *But we will remember the name of the*
> *LORD our God.*
> *They have bowed down and fallen;*
> *But we have risen and stand upright.*
> —PS. 20:7–8

I first met Brian at a meeting. He was very depressed, expressing the desire that the Lord would come soon and end his struggles. As we talked, I learned that he had been unable to stay sober, that he was bitter about his church and his God, feeling they had both let him down. He simply wanted to quit, to end it all. He was without hope or faith.

Slowly at first, then more quickly, Brian began to see the difference between the quantity of his faith and its quality. He had been religious, but not really faithful. As he grew in faith, he feared less. And he became hopeful, seeing the forest instead of just the trees.

Today Brian serves as an example to others. He is entering seminary this fall, answering the call of God. And my faith has grown as well, for God has given me the opportunity to see another of His life-changing miracles up close.

God, thank You for Your ability to strengthen me as I reach out with feeble faith. Help me to grow in faith and to fear less.

T. S.

But each one is tempted when he is drawn away by his own desires and enticed. —JAMES 1:14

A very thin line lies between sexual temptation and sin. As men we are all faced with sexual temptation daily—while working, watching television, reading a magazine, or even going to a shopping mall. In fact, since we are all physically attracted to women, not to be might in some circles be considered abnormal. When, though, does mental attraction to a woman become a sin?

Temptation is transformed into lust when we allow an original sexual thought to preoccupy us. A sexual feeling or thought in itself is not wrong. Sexual temptation is looking at an attractive woman once; sin is looking twice.

What then can we do as men to control our lustful sexual desires? The Bible says that the wise man will flee from sin. If we train our eyes not to wander, maybe our minds will not ponder. When we purposefully take an eyeful of the cute girl walking by, we are only taking a risk. And we can learn to notice other things about women—personality, spiritual gifts, intelligence, and talents.

———————

Lord, help me not to raise my eyebrow.

L. S.

The ear that hears the reproof of life
Will abide among the wise.
—PROV. 15:31

No one likes to be confronted. We don't want to hear about our shortcomings or mistakes. Usually we become defensive or even hostile toward the person who is pointing them out.

It has been said that in any criticism or confrontation there lies the potential for at least a nugget of truth. I once worked for a very demanding employer. He was often critical of the work his employees did. The employees felt a lot of anger and hostility towards him. One day, it was my turn. As he was commenting in a very angry way about the job that I had been doing, I remember practicing this truth. While most of what he said was out of proportion and untrue, I did find a small nugget of truth that actually helped me improve the job that I was performing.

Wisdom comes from being open to hearing the rebukes that may come in our lives. While anger may be our initial reaction, it is important to evaluate the confrontation and heed any wisdom that might be included in the message.

Lord, give me the strength to be open to criticisms and the wisdom to acknowledge truth.

B. N.

I would have lost heart, unless I had believed.
—PS. 27:13

When I first got to AA, I knew everything. When my sponsor told me that it was what I learned that was going to help me, I didn't understand what he meant.

The second step was a mystery unknown to me then. I thought it was obvious: you couldn't get from Step 1 to Step 3 unless Step 2 was there. That was its purpose. You can imagine how puzzled I was when Carter related his story.

It seems that Carter's life hadn't improved much after he was sober one year. His sponsor told him to work the second step. After Carter was sober two years, his life still wasn't much better, and his sponsor said, "Work the second step." Imagine my confusion when I heard this: I thought the second step didn't have a purpose.

Today the second step is very important to me. It's the place where my fear is replaced by faith, where my doubt is replaced by assurance.

Lord, thank You for what I learned after I knew everything. Please continue to give me examples like Carter to stretch my thinking about You.

T. S.

> *Do not let your heart turn aside to her ways,*
> *Do not stray into her paths;*
> *For she has cast down many wounded,*
> *And all who were slain by her were strong men.*
> —PROV. 7:25–26

We have all heard that prostitution is one of the oldest professions. Women have been profiting from male sexuality for thousands of years. Some men pay up to five hundred dollars just for one hour with a high-dollar call girl.

Men today somehow sense an inward warning about being with a prostitute. Our consciences tell us that we are approaching something forbidden. Even so the inner voice fails to keep many from being lured into the trap.

What force lures a man toward a prostitute? Loneliness. Most men frequent prostitutes not for the sex, but for intimacy. For a man sex equals love and is his primary love source. Although a man is led to believe that all of his needs will be satisfied in a contracted sexual encounter, he actually comes out of the experience empty and ashamed.

Prostitution reduces sexuality to a mere mechanical physical act, sex without love, mutual masturbation. It falls short of God's design for human sexuality—the bonding of a man and woman in a one-partner, one-flesh relationship.

Lord, may You keep me from the lure of strange women.

L. S.

Hold fast what is good.
—1 THESS. 5:21

When I started playing golf, I didn't take it seriously, nor did I think there was much game in hitting a stationary white ball the size of a hailstone. As my love for the game grew, I found that I didn't quite understand or appreciate its finer points—one of them being consistency. I thought that by sheer power I could master this game. Wrong!

In one of my first rounds of golf, I was paired with a man in his early eighties. I let him tee off first. He hit it straight down the middle of the fairway, but only 100 yards. My tee shot went 250 yards. This was of no help because hitting a ball 250 yards due west is of little value when the hole is 375 yards straight north. In four straight, consistent, short shots the elderly man was on the green putting for bogey. In four long, erratic shots, I was struggling to stay in the same time zone. The problem? Lack of consistency.

Do you try to control life by your own strength or by knowing your limitations and striving for consistency? God doesn't want flair but a life that is patient and guided by a straight path. How's your consistency? How's your game?

Father, I humble myself before You, knowing my strength lies in You. Teach me the discipline of consistency.

B. D.

> *Jesus said . . . , "No one, having put his hand to the plow, and looking back, is fit for the kingdom of God."*
>
> —LUKE 9:62

On his hundredth birthday, a well-known cynic was interviewed by the local newspaper. The young reporter, expecting to tap a lifetime of experience, asked: "In a hundred years, Mr. Smith, you must have seen many new things."

"Yes," the old man replied, "and I was against every one of them!"

Since I first fell into Twelve-Step fellowship, I've struggled with closed-mindedness. My initial reaction to something new is, "No, that can't possibly work." And I am consistently wrong. When I refuse new things, I frequently am tempted to look back. Here are some ways to keep looking forward:

1. Stick with the winners (those who stay sober, who will lead you forward), not the losers.

2. Stay away from old friends (the ones who may not be good for you), and make new friends.

3. Do the next right thing. If you don't know what that is, ask someone who does.

Dear God, help me to open my mind to Your better way of living and thinking today.

T. S.

He who walks with wise men will be wise,
But the companion of fools will be destroyed.
—PROV. 13:20

I would never have made it through my own recovery without my mentor. My mentor or role model encouraged and guided me throughout my early recovery. My mentor was bigger than life; he was the bedrock of stability; he reflected for me what normal was; and he gleamed with inner strength and integrity. He gave me a reason to hope and a goal to work toward.

A mentor is valuable when a man is seriously undertaking his recovery. No one has ever recovered totally on his own from an addiction. In recovery it is important to align oneself with a healthy role model, a model to look up to.

A mentor is usually older and wiser, someone who has faced his problems head on and came out as a stronger man on the other side. He is someone you deeply trust. A mentor is one who is willing to take you on as an apprentice, working with you until you have learned the trade of life. Most importantly, a mentor walks closely with God.

Lord, I pray that You will bring me a mentor who walks after You.

L. S.

> *As iron sharpens iron,*
> *So a man sharpens the*
> *countenance of his friend.*
> —PROV. 27:17

Every man needs another man to look him straight in the eye and ask him the hard questions of life. How is your spiritual life? How is your thought life? How are your relationships with your family? What does it really mean to be a man of integrity in a world of getting ahead? Is being married and remaining faithful to your wife really worth the hassle? Do my kids really need interaction with me? What really makes life worthwhile? It's easy to hide when we don't have another man to be accountable to.

Do you have another man you can spend time with, asking the tough questions of life? Without this kind of man in your life, you are sure to grow dull. Just as iron sharpens iron, man sharpens man.

Try an experiment. Have lunch or spend a short time today with another man, and ask one or two of those questions.

_____

Lord, sharpen me today as I reach out to sharpen others.

B. N.

Better is a little with the fear of the LORD,
Than great treasure with trouble.
—PROV. 15:16

Rich was a very successful pharmacist. With two drug stores and many employees, he literally made more money than he could count. That's because he was drunk or under the influence of drugs most of the time.

When Rich got to AA, he had lost everything except his house and his wife. One year later, drinking again, he lost his house. Several years later, beaten and broken, Rich finally admitted he was powerless and came to believe God could restore him to sanity.

Convinced that he could not resume his profession because of the availability of drugs, Rich took a job as a gardener in a local park, where he still works. He lives in a smaller, new house with his wife. He enjoys his grandchild. He lives life one day at a time, having realized that a little with God as his friend is better than riches with trouble.

Lord, let me appreciate the advantages of life as Your friend. Thank You for Your wise provision for all my needs.

T. S.

Putting away lying, each one speak truth with his neighbor, for we are members of one another.
—EPH. 4:25

Whatever happened to male integrity? We seem to have to look far and wide to find an honest and upright man. In earlier times two men used to close big business deals with a handshake and a stern look in the eyes. If a man gave his word, he considered it sacred.

The age of honest men is far behind us. We commonly read about sex scandals, tax crimes, college recruiting violations, and contract violations on almost every page of the paper. No one is trusted anymore. There must be lawyers and contracts for every deal; extensive credit checks are run on consumers; and background investigations are run on public officials to see if they've committed any crimes. This is a time of lie detectors, watchdog groups, and ethics committees.

I believe that the major reason so many men have lost their integrity is for the cause of money, power, and sex. Man has an insatiable appetite for these things and violates his own value system to get them, never thinking of the consequences.

We Christian men need to work toward having more integrity. We need to live in accordance with God's standards and our own value system. If we are beyond reproach in all our dealings, we can more easily live with ourselves one day at a time.

It can take a lifetime to gain your integrity, and you can lose it in a second.

L. S.

*Persecuted, but not forsaken; struck down, but
not destroyed.*   —2 COR. 4:9

Many people suffer a trauma that compounds the
pain they are already feeling and lends itself to despair.
Often, the alcoholic who is working through recovery
is keenly aware of the problems his drinking has
caused. The family, feeling their own abandonment
and pain, often reject the alcoholic. To the alcoholic
there is a sense of salt being heaped on the wound.
Being rejected and forsaken by others, especially family, has a way of pinning him to the ground. Where
does he turn? Who hears his cry?

There is hope; there is someone. His name is Jesus.

In the course of a lifetime and in the process of recovery, one may feel the pain of rejection, the sting of
persecution. There are also times in the process that
one will fall and not have the strength to battle back
up. Through the darkness we can know someone is
there. Jesus walks with the persecuted and holds the
forsaken. Even as we feel downtrodden, we can still
look up to victory.

While man may continually reject you, God offers
acceptance and love through Christ Jesus. You are not
alone.

———————

*Lord, in my humanness I will fall. Thank You for lifting me and hold-
ing me close.*

B. D.

> *My grace is sufficient for you, for My strength is*
> *made perfect in weakness.*   —2 COR. 12:9

I wasn't afraid of anything. I wasn't allowed. My dad's order to me was, "Don't get angry, don't cry, and don't be afraid." And so I wasn't . . . unless I was drunk!

After I got to AA, I heard how fear was behind my every negative feeling, negative reaction, and character defect. You can imagine how puzzled I was; I wasn't afraid of anything, and yet fear was behind all my problems—a dilemma that would last for two years.

One evening, as I heard a young man speak of his fear, I suddenly realized that I was afraid . . . of everything. That night I wrote a list of fourteen primary fears and prayed about them. As I continued to acknowledge my fears, the Lord provided faith to deal with each of them. God's grace is truly sufficient as I learn and relearn that my powerlessness over my fears provides me with strength to overcome them.

Lord, thank You for providing Your strength to me. I pray that I may grow strong as I continue to confess my fears to You.

T. S.

As iron sharpens iron,
So a man sharpens
the countenance of his friend.
—PROV. 27:17

Most men would admit that they would like to be total masters of their own lives. They would want to have their own businesses, make all of their own decisions, and work out their own problems. The roots of this fantasy among men lie in the need to be in control and the tendency to foster macho pride.

As you continue to examine yourself, remember that some of the most successful men of our age have been listeners. Jesus himself sought God's wisdom daily and hourly. When we fail to listen to others, we begin to deprive ourselves of opportunities for inner growth.

In choosing those men with whom you will yield yourself to regular accountability, you should look for several qualities. These men should walk closely with God, have integrity beyond reproach, and have your respect. They should love order in their own lives and not be afraid to speak the truth about any problems they detect in your life.

Lord, help me to know what I am—to other men and to You.

L. S.

Go therefore and make disciples of all the nations.
—MATT. 28:19

There are so many concerns in our world. Nuclear waste, AIDS, saving the whales, paper or plastic. Ecuador is racing against time to save its tropical forests.

All of these to one degree or another affect our well-being. But where do I place them on my priority list, and does that list take up the cause of Christ?

Proclaiming the gospel and making disciples has more impact than all other issues especially as they relate to the future—eternity.

We should all do our utmost to protect God's earth and show compassion for the sick. But the priority must be changing lives for eternity. Millions have died untouched by the gospel. Countless more may die untouched because the believer chooses a cause believed to be greater than the souls of men.

Remember, our primary cause is Christ's mandate.

Lord, move me to be bold in my witness and true in my convictions. May my cause be the gospel; my motivation, my love for You.

B. D.

"Your daughter is dead. Why trouble the Teacher any further?" As soon as Jesus heard the word that was spoken, He said to the ruler of the synagogue, "Do not be afraid; only believe."

—MARK 5:35–36

I have heard this story of Jesus restoring the little girl to life many times in church. Maybe you have, too. If so, I'm sure you were told how the story illustrated Jesus' power over death, how clearly Jesus' humility and lovingkindness show through. Perhaps I wasn't listening, but I don't remember hearing about what my part should be: "Do not be afraid; only believe."

That little world *only* may mean one of two things:

1. Begin with your entry level faith.
2. Trusting Jesus is all we need to do. It's enough!

I believe that both are true. So when I'm afraid, rather than whistling a happy tune, I try instead to remember Jesus' instruction. I try to believe, only believe. And as I try, the image of Jesus, loving and kind, powerful even over death, comes to my mind. And guess what? I'm not so afraid anymore.

Loving Lord Jesus, remind me of Your love for me when I am afraid. Assure me of Your power and strength to handle all situations, as You did for the little girl and her family.

T. S.

Therefore let him who thinks he stands take heed lest he fall.
—1 COR. 10:12

Proverbs 16:25 says,

There is a way that seems right to a man,
But its end is the way of death.

This is true for a man on the treacherous road of recovery. I am warning of the problem of pride. A prideful man in recovery is like a man attempting a tightrope walk across a deep canyon blindfolded and on one foot. Many of the world's best have fallen off the road of recovery to their deaths because of their pride. An addiction does not care who you are; how rich you are; how intelligent you are; or how much willpower you have. So pride has no redeeming value in recovery.

Pride is deadly. It keeps the man in recovery from seeing the dangers of small risks with his addiction. It keeps a man from seeking help from others who are walking the same road and from seeing his own character defects. Most importantly, pride separates a man from God, which is the lifeline of his recovery.

Lord, teach me to be humble.

L. S.

Chasten your son while there is hope,
And do not set your heart on his destruction.
—PROV. 19:18

Not many fathers set out to destroy their children's lives. But too many fathers don't realize until it's too late that their lack of involvement has been doing this all along. Monty didn't think about the impact of his work habits on his children until he was forty-nine and his third child ran away at sixteen. She was out on the streets somewhere after he had labored all her life to provide a luxurious home in the right neighborhood, with a swimming pool and promise of her own car. At first it made no sense. She must be crazy to choose a life on the streets rather than with him.

A child needs a father's consistency. Children need their fathers to be consistent in love, discipline, presence, and nurturing.

Discipline is important for children. Fathers need to be committed to provide it. It's not just the mother's job. Your children will grow to be strong, healthy individuals as you practice involvement through not just providing the roof over their heads, but the discipline and love they long for. Remember, someday it will be too late.

Be a consistent dad while there is still time.

B. N.

*Made a decision to turn our will and our lives over
to the care of God as we understood Him.*
—THE TWELVE STEPS OF ALCOHOLICS ANONYMOUS

*Most assuredly, I say to you, he who hears My word
and believes in Him who sent Me has everlasting
life, and shall not come into judgment, but has
passed from death into life.*   —JOHN 5:24

Kurt called me yesterday. He had his driver's license
and had bought a used car. He was really excited. But
last night his battery died, and he was upset. All this is
new to Kurt, so he's relying on his friends to coach
him.

I've known Kurt for almost ten years. He stayed with
me several times. I visited him in hospitals and treatment centers. Blinded by selfishness, he couldn't visu-
alize, wouldn't accept, a loving God who would show
him mercy and grace.

Two years ago, something happened—I don't know
what exactly—whatever it takes for a man to change
his mind. Kurt changed his mind about God.

First, there was the hospital, then the halfway house,
and now Kurt lives on his own. As time passes, he is
less selfish, less afraid, more assured of God's love. It
was good hearing from Kurt.

*Thank You for Your work in Kurt's life and all the men we know like
him. Men like us.*

T. S.

*The drunkard and the glutton will come to poverty,
And drowsiness will clothe a man with rags.*
—PROV. 23:21

Abraham Maslow addressed human personality in terms of a hierarchy of needs. According to him, man had the following needs in this order: food, water, safety, security, belongingness, love, and self-actualization. Thus personality develops around a capacity and drive to meet these needs. The problem of gluttony or the drive to satiate oneself is born out of our most primitive dependency needs.

As infants we all have three basic needs—nourishment, love, and security. Men who were fed appropriately, held regularly, and protected consistently as infants tend to become secure and stable adults. Men who were not fed when hungry, were left alone for long periods of time, and were not well nurtured tend to become insecure and extremely dependent.

A man whose nurturing needs were not met may turn to food, alcohol, or drugs for security and thus create an addictive cycle. To get off this merry-go-round is like cutting a lifeline.

The man who struggles with gluttony has to learn how to set limits on what he takes into his body. This is not easy since it threatens his very survival. He makes limits for himself by delaying gratification on a gradual basis. As he learns that he can do without and still be okay, he can then transfer this principle to other areas of his life.

———

Lord, help me to practice moderation.

L. S.

> *But the hour is coming, and now is, when the*
> *true worshipers will worship the Father in spirit*
> *and truth; for the Father is seeking such to*
> *worship Him.*
> —JOHN 4:23

Quality time. For so long I thought this was an over-used cliché. Then I had a child of my own. My little boy is growing and changing so quickly I have a desire to spend time with him. This time must have quality. I become in tune with my son when I can physically communicate and interact, one to one.

Right now the world is new to him, and he is learning who I am. He looks to me for comfort and help. There is never a question in his mind about whether Daddy will come through.

As each day goes by, our time together becomes more special, more "quality." The more we share, the greater the relationship grows. He wants me, and I want to be with him. How much more "quality" can there be?

Our heavenly Father desires a similar relationship with each of us. God is our comforter and teacher. We can run to Him when we're hurt, happy, or sad. This "Daddy" always comes through. Here is real quality.

Father, keep me ever mindful of my need to spend time with You.

B. D.

*And this is the will of Him who sent Me, that every
one who sees the Son and believes in Him may
have everlasting life; and I will raise him up at
the last day.* —JOHN 6:40

A group of seminary students were using the gym
late one evening. The janitor had come to open the
doors and sat quietly by the door reading his Bible.

One of the students—young, bright, and knowing
everything as only young men can—walked over to
the old man and asked what he was doing. "Readin'
my Bible," replied the janitor.

"Do you understand it?" asked the student.

"Yep," answered the old man.

"All of it?" the younger man grinned.

"Yep," was the reply.

Stretching to his full height, the student asked, "And
just what does it say?"

"It says," the janitor smiled, "we win!"

The spirit of the third step lies in the assurance that
because of our decision to turn our will and life over to
God's care, we win.

---

*Sovereign, all-powerful Lord, remind us today that our eternal life
with You has already begun. Remind us that our physical death is
merely an event in a wonderful life with You.*

T. S.

> *But I say to you that whoever looks at a woman to lust for her has already committed adultery with her in his heart.*
> —MATT. 5:28

The next time you look at a woman and undress her in your mind, think for a moment how you would feel if some other man was having the same thoughts about your wife or a woman who is dear to you and your family. How does it feel even now as you're thinking about what I'm saying? Do you feel some guilt? We all do since we know instinctively that we are walking on forbidden territory. As men we somehow rationalize or justify committing sins of the heart. Some of the common rationalizations I've heard are, "It's better than actually doing it," "If women wouldn't dress so provocatively, I wouldn't have to lust," and "It's normal—all men do it."

Men can find no escape from this temptation to lust after women. There is also no escape from our personal responsibility to be good stewards with our sexuality. How can we manage the power of our sexuality and live out our sexuality in a way that is pleasing to God?

First, we must be willing to submit our wills in the area of our sexual desire to God. Then we must train our eyes not to look into forbidden zones. Just one look can be immobilizing. Third, realize that lust will eventually not be enough; then acting out will be inevitable.

Lord, help me not to be drawn away and enticed by my own lust.

L. S.

*He who mistreats his father and chases away
  his mother
Is a son who causes shame and brings reproach.*
—PROV. 19:26

It is important for men to recognize the importance of their role as son in the family. Some men may have every logical right to never unite with their parents again because of abuse or other issues, but all men *are* sons and need to be accountable for their decisions as sons. God's Word instructs men to honor their parents.

The story of Cain in the Bible is the first example of a son bringing shame to his family. Cain was so jealous of his brother that he killed him. What you do with your life today affects other people.

God can help you best understand how to honor and respect your parents even if they are not honorable or respectable. Honoring your parents brings freedom to your life from the bondage of bitterness. Sons also must be careful not to become overly dependent on their parents as a source of approval. Codependency on parents is not honoring them.

If your parents are still living, make a point of calling or writing them today to let them know you love and care for them.

Help me to live a life that honors my parents.

B. N.

But let your "Yes" be "Yes," and your "No," "No."
For whatever is more than these is from the
evil one. —MATT. 5:37

A farmer hired a workman to do some jobs around the farm. The first job was to put up some fence. The farmer figured it would take a day. The workman was done by noon.

The next job was to paint the barn. The farmer expected it to take a week. The workman was done in three days.

The third job was to sort the newly dug potatoes into three piles: one for the potatoes to go to market, a second for seed for the new crop, and a third pile for poor potatoes, fit only to feed the pigs. The farmer thought it should take a day, but when he returned, the workman was standing by three pitifully small piles, dwarfed by a huge pile of unsorted potatoes.

"Hey!" said the farmer. "What's the problem here?"

"Oh, I can work pretty good," said the workman, "but I can't make decisions."

The decision part of the third step caused me problems. But one day, I decided to learn how to let God handle my life. So far, it's been okay. How's it been with you? _____

Heavenly Father, help us to take a minute today to see how we're doing in honoring the decision to turn our lives and will over to You.

T. S.

> *Submit to God. Resist the devil and he will flee*
> *from you.* —JAMES 4:7

There are five basic phases of recovery from an addiction or compulsive behavior. The first phase is denial—bottoming out, but not seeing it. In phase two, bargaining, a man maintains alternate addictions to avoid the reality of abstinence. Phase three is verbal but not necessarily heartfelt admission of the problem. Phase four is acceptance, and surrender is the final stage.

Acceptance and surrender are miles apart. At the point of acceptance a man acknowledges his problem out of submissive compliance. He says defiantly, "All right, I have a problem, but I'm going to beat it."

In the fifth phase a man surrenders to the addiction in his body, soul, mind, and spirit. He says, "I admit that I'm powerless and that only God can deliver me from my addiction one day at a time."

What phase of recovery are you in? If you are at the point of surrender, you'll feel a letting go and an inner peace.

Surrender is the point at which a man quits fighting life and goes with it.

L. S.

> *Because it is written, "Be holy, for I am holy."*
> —1 PETER 1:16

In a world that leaves little room for error, men are driven by the pursuit of perfection. We must be perfect to get ahead, be noticed, reach the top. But what about reality? Can we reach perfection? My own bias says no. Perfection gives no room for anything but 1000 percent. No blemishes, no minute deviance, no "almosts." Perfection is not forgiving.

Too many in today's culture are not realists when it comes to establishing their ultimate goal.

Let me offer an alternative. There is still a lot of work involved, but we can "settle" for excellence. Excellence is a conscious striving for the best. It recognizes that I am not perfect. Oh what freedom, oh what relief!

In God's holy Word we are called to be holy. We will not fully realize this until we see Christ and become as He is (1 John 3:1–3). But we will strive for holiness, for excellence. Are you shackled by the lie of perfection, or are you free to pursue excellence?

Lord, I am but a man. I am not perfect, but move me to excellence.

B. D.

The helpless commits himself to You;
You are the helper of the fatherless.
—PS. 10:14

When I was a boy, I read the funny papers every Sunday. I remember one "Beetle Bailey" strip in particular where Sarge is talking to the men, asking them to look on him as a father, as if the platoon were one big, happy family. Beetle offers this aside: "If Sarge was my father, I'd become a professional orphan."

I grew up in a dysfunctional family, where normal conversation began at eighty decibels and went up from there. I fantasized about what it would be like to be in my friends' families.

This verse assures me that God wants me to be fathered and provides men to stand in His place and father me. He did that for me through a small group. These other men mentor, encourage, and direct me as I grow up in Christ.

God, thank You for providing men to father me. Help me to be the right kind of dad for my children.

T. S.

> *Let every man be swift to hear, slow to speak, slow to wrath; for the wrath of man does not produce the righteousness of God.* —JAMES 1:19–20

John was an angry man, constantly yelling at his wife and children. On the highway John rebuffed those who drove too slow or too fast. In arguments at work with various supervisors, though, he had to conceal his anger to avoid being fired.

Why was John so angry? Were his family and employer out to sabotage his life and make him miserable? No, John had a problem with displaced anger, placing the anger on the wrong person or object because it is safer. In John's case it was safer for him to get angry at his wife and kids than to tangle with his supervisor.

There is an easy to way to know if you have a problem with displaced anger. If you express your anger and it persists, then it is probably displaced. Displaced anger will never go away until it is returned to its source.

Lord, show me the true origins of my wrath.

L. S.

There is nothing better for a man than that he should eat and drink, and that his soul should enjoy good in his labor. —ECCL. 2:24

Recently, I had a chance to visit with an old friend. We talked about all the things God had been doing in our lives. We discussed our career paths and wondered at the ways we had been successful and blessed by God. It wasn't a time of bragging or trying to outdo the other. It was a time of being thankful and praising God for the wonderful things He had done for us.

It is important for men to stop and evaluate the impact they are having on their world. God wants us to feel good and satisfied in the successes He has provided. Men have a drive to feel adequate, that they are making a difference. This is a God-given need.

It is easy to look at your shortcomings and your unreached goals, but this brings a lot of discouragement. God wants you to enjoy success. He wants you to be thankful to Him for helping to provide it. My friend and I hardly feel that we have "made it," but it sure is nice to look back and feel good about what we have accomplished.

_____

God, help me to acknowledge the success You give me today.

B. N.

> *But let your "Yes" be "Yes," and your "No," "No,"*
> *lest you fall into judgment.* —JAMES 5:12

I don't know, Marty . . . What do you want to do?"

"I don't know, Angie . . . What do you want to do?"

These lines, spoken over and over, provoked great laughter in the play *Marty*. There is something very funny about the inability to make a decision.

I never wanted to make a decision because decision brought responsibility. What if I decided what we do for fun and it wasn't fun? I'd be responsible. What if I decided to buy a certain stock and the market crashed? It would be my fault!

When I came to AA, I was soon asked to decide to turn my will and my life over to the care of God! That's a big decision, so I put it off. The need to make a decision did not go away, however, so three years after I came to believe that God could help me, I formally asked Him to take charge of my will and my life.

Guess what? It turned out to be the right decision. God has never let me down! And I have been freed to make other decisions with just a little less difficulty.

God, help me to affirm my total dependence upon You today. Free me so that my decisions are deliberate and unchanging.

T. S.

He who is slow to wrath has great understanding,
But he who is impulsive exalts folly.
—PROV. 14:29

Anger and work tend to be inseparable. There is often no healthy outlet for anger at work. Others make the decisions that affect us. Coworkers who are not actually over us act as if they are, telling us what to do, when and how to do it, and how we did it wrong. It is also difficult for us to get what we feel we are entitled to at work.

How then are we to deal with our anger and resentment at work? We don't want to react in aggressive or controlling ways. Aggression at work is normally met with punishment or termination.

The key to handling anger at work is to prevent it. We can avoid anger by decreasing our entitlement and expectations, realizing that our employer doesn't owe us anything and is not likely to consider our needs first. We can decide not to internalize or personalize; everything that happens at work is not about us. And we can assert ourselves wisely and turn the rest of our anger over to God one day at a time.

No anger is better than unbridled anger.

L. S.

> *For the law was given through Moses, but grace and truth came through Jesus Christ.*
>
> —JOHN 1:17

There seems to be something different about vibrant believers in Christ Jesus. They have joy and laughter that results from a clear understanding of grace and the finished work of the Cross.

What a gloomy picture we often paint when we buy into the lie that Christianity is dull. There is nothing dull about grace, but we don't really appreciate it unless we understand it. Understanding grace and its liberating power should provide all the joy we need to enjoy life and share our joy.

What keeps us from experiencing joy and inhibits our living? Let me suggest three things. First, the sin that so easily entangles us (Heb. 12:1). Unconfessed sin is like chains wrapped around our feet. The joy of victory can't truly be experienced if we're too bound up to run the race. Second, not fully realizing that grace has made us brand new. There is no need to be haunted by our past. We are new creatures in Christ (2 Cor. 5:17). Third, learning to "loosen up." Too often, we're consumed with pleasing God when we should be enjoying Him. Grace has set us free to experience joy—the joy found only in Christ Jesus.

Lord, it was grace that set me free. I praise You for the gift of joy and eternal life.

B. D.

*The LORD also will be a refuge
for the oppressed,
A refuge in times of trouble.*
—PS. 9:9

I take great comfort in God's promise to me to be a refuge in time of trouble. But it was not always so. After three years in AA, I questioned whether the gospel story was true. I had questions: Is Jesus really alive today and at God's right hand, or is this just a fable?

Pardon my demanding bluntness, but I asked God, if He existed, to show Himself. And He did! Oh, not in the ways He did to Moses at Sinai, to be sure. But He consistently heard my prayers, led me to people who could help me, and provided comfort at times when my life was not going well.

How did He do it? Through the wise people who have walked with Him for many years, whose counsel is backed up with life experience, who are what I call "God with skin on." They model Christ for me, encouraging, sharing, and helping as I seek to know Him better.

Lord, thank You for the wise people in my life who model Christ for me. Help me to become one of them so that I may help and encourage others.

T. S.

> *I sought the Lord, and He heard me,*
> *And delivered me from all my fears.*
> —PS. 34:4

Anxiety always comes upon me when I least expect it. Suddenly a terrible tingling and paralysis sensation pervades my body—as though I just walked into an electrical field. I cannot shake anxiety off immediately and run from it or repress it. But it won't be ignored.

Anxiety renders a man powerless over his emotional and physical comfort. And fear is the active ingredient, fear of the unknown or of loss. Since its origin is usually a mystery, we must live with it until a medicine relieves it or until we can talk ourselves out of it.

When you face anxiety, avoid medication unless a doctor recommends it. A tranquilizer may offer temporary relief from the feeling, but it doesn't deal with the origin. Realize that your body may be telling you that you need to face a problem. Try listening to relaxation techniques, correcting your self-talk, and meditating on Scripture.

Lord, help me to cast my care upon You in trust.

L. S.

Go from the presence of a foolish man,
When you do not perceive in him the lips
of knowledge. —PROV. 14:7

It is easy to find a group of men who are not walking in a godly manner. You may find yourself with such men at the office, at the sports club, anywhere.

A friend of mine told me about a recent trip to the golf course. Tom was in a foursome with a group of influential men whose conversation was deteriorating with each hole they finished. He had a choice to stay and listen, to speak up, or to leave. When Tom shared his feelings about the level of conversation, the others became hostile and defensive. Tom figured it wasn't worth listening to the garbage through the final nine holes, so he left. It was a tough choice. Just because Tom could recognize the men as fools in their manner of conversation, he didn't want to be thought badly of by anyone, not even by a fool.

The need not to appear "too Christian" or "too different" leads many men to stay around the fools and sometimes to fall into trouble. God suggests that we leave, lest the foolishness rub off on us. It takes courage to run from fools.

Lord, help me not be a fool. Give me the wisdom to know when I need to run from fools.

B. N.

> *The fear of the LORD is the beginning of wisdom.*
> —PS. 111:10

I grew up with a misshapen view of God. To me He was a cosmic killjoy, wanting me always to be a good little boy and behave. I can't blame the church I went to or even my parents, but somehow it just came to me that God was to be feared. Verses like the one above supported that viewpoint. In short, God was out to get me!

Today, I understand the verse differently. Fear has more to do with respecting God's perfect law, His perfect plan for me, and His provision for me in Jesus Christ. Understanding what God wants me to do and say and taking that as a goal toward which I strive is what fear of the Lord is for me. And that is the beginning of wisdom.

I doubt if I will ever be truly wise in God's sight, but it is my goal to get as close as I can, day by day, to the knowledge and assurance of His plan for my life.

God, thank You for Your love for me as shown in Jesus Christ. Help me to understand that plan and grow in wisdom today.

T. S.

Whoever hides hatred has lying lips,
And whoever spreads slander is a fool.
—PROV. 10:18

When we go to work, we almost have to shield our backs. Everywhere we turn someone is saying something questionable about us. I'm sure you know who it is that may come up and bite you in the back. Of course, you and I would never do that.

Why do backbiters live on lies about others? They are insecure. They constantly build themselves up by putting others down. They must constantly be number one at work, fearing that they won't succeed unless they wipe out their competition. Backbiters are scared of others, so they passively share their feelings by spiting you behind your back.

If you work with a backbiter, you can do some things to protect your back. First, avoid contact with the backbiter; never tell him anything personal. If you make sure that someone above him knows you, likes you, and knows your heart, he cannot sabotage your job. Finally, do not place yourself in his shoes, or people will feel about you the same way they feel about him.

Lord, help me to be a man that others trust and in whom others confide.

L. S.

*Set your mind on things above, not on things
on the earth.*
—COL. 3:2

Have you ever wondered what it must feel like to make three million dollars a year? What does it take to be of that much value? For many hardworking professional baseball players this salary is a reality.

The very best hitters in baseball get three hits for every ten at bat, and they usually average about .330 for a given year. Once in a great while someone comes along and bats .400. Imagine your boss saying, "Mr. Smith, we see that you accomplished three out of ten goals this year, and you deserve a huge raise." We must, however, live in reality. Reality dictates that doing only 30 percent of your job wins you an extended vacation and a pink slip.

Teachers across this land are changing professions because of a lack of money for education. Police officers often work overtime to make ends meet. Churches struggle as 20 percent of the congregation maintains 80 percent of the budget.

As believers we are entrusted with God's money to be faithful stewards. We place value on the work of our Lord, who gave 100 percent.

Lord, I pray that my mind and heart will be set on imperishable things with eternal value.

B. D.

How long, O LORD? Will You forget me forever?
How long will You hide Your face from me?
—PS. 13:1

My third year in AA was the worst for me, so far. Life had become boring, I didn't have the things I thought I needed, and I was in bondage to myself. I thought that God had let me down. I had been good, had worked at spiritual growth, and was ready for a "promotion" to a better lifestyle.

When it became obvious that things were not changing for me in the areas of sex, status, and security, I decided I had had enough and went back to handling things myself. What happened? The wheels came off my life. The serenity I had achieved with God's help disappeared. After eight months on what is called a "dry drunk," I gave up.

After an emotional exchange with a friend, I got into my car and sped away, not knowing where I should go. When I reached the corner, I could turn right to go home and call for help or turn left and go to the liquor store. I turned right.

Shortly thereafter I really made the decision to let God have control of my will and life. And my life did improve. God has provided for me beyond my wildest dreams—not with everything I want, but with everything I need.

God, thank You for providing things that are good for me. Direct my life today as I seek to do Your will.

T. S.

Watch and pray, lest you enter into temptation. The spirit indeed is willing, but the flesh is weak.
—MATT. 26:41

John was a thirty-year-old alcoholic. He had been out of treatment for four weeks when he came in and told me he had relapsed. "I don't understand what happened," he said. "I've been going to my AA meetings and working Steps One, Two, and Three faithfully."

As we talked, John came to see that his relapse occurred because of two errors in his working of Step Three.

First, John realized that turning over his will and his life meant he had to turn over his behavior, as well as his mind to God. John gave God his will with his mind, but he would still walk by taverns, focus on liquor advertisements, and drive through neighborhoods where he used to drink.

Second, John realized that turning over his will was not a one-time event. John had thought he could turn over his will with a prayer in the morning and that it would last twenty-four hours.

Lord, help me to turn my life and will over to you one step at a time.
L. S.

A time to weep, And a time to laugh;
A time to mourn, And a time to dance . . .
—ECCL. 3:4

Traditionally men have been brought up not to be emotional. The message received by most boys is that "real men don't cry." King Solomon reminds us that we need to acknowledge our emotions. Sometimes we need to weep and sometimes we need to laugh. Dancing and mourning are all a part of our human existence.

Harry was so out of touch with his emotions that it drove the most important people in his world away from him. He was like a crying baby trapped behind thick prison walls, and he couldn't even let those tears out to save his marriage. Harry and Marge had been coming to counseling, but Harry would never open up. The day he came home to find their house empty, he called for an emergency session. When he finally let out what he was feeling inside, he cried like a baby for five minutes. Those tears were the beginning of changing his marriage into an intimate bond that both he and his wife needed.

We serve a God who is emotional. We were created in His image as emotional beings. If we buy into the belief that real men don't cry, we must lock up an important part of ourselves.

God, give me the strength to be honest with my emotions.

B. N.

Better is a neighbor nearby than a
brother far away.
—PROV. 27:10

Yesterday I began another business trip. As I walked alone through the St. Louis airport, I felt that now-familiar loneliness, almost smallness I always feel as I get my bags alone, rent my car alone, and check into a hotel room alone. It's not that people are unkind. The flight crew, the rental clerk, the desk clerk all call me by name, are kind and helpful . . . but they don't know me! There is no one I know waiting for me.

When I return home in a few days, I will feel different. I'll get my bags, get a ride home, all similar stuff to yesterday, but with a difference. Someone is waiting for me! Someone is counting on my return, so it matters whether I get home. I am important to them!

I realize, too, that my friends are like me, that sometimes they need me to wait for them. They count on me to tell them they matter by waiting at the airport. We all need someone waiting for us at the station.

Lord, thank You for friends who wait for me. Please help me to appreciate and look for chances You give me to "wait at the station" for my friends.

T. S.

*With us is the LORD our God, to help us and to
fight our battles.* —2 CHRON. 32:8

Sam had been at his sales job for five years. He was
dissatisfied with the way he was treated. Sam felt he
was always the guy who had to work weekends. People kept smoking around him. He had received little
financial increase over five years. His one promotion
just involved more work at almost the same pay. The
men he worked with ribbed him all the time and used
him.

Sam's problems were really the result of his lack of
boundaries, limits set to protect his integrity and well-being. Sam had no physical boundaries; he allowed
people to smoke next to him without saying anything.
He also had no spiritual boundaries. He allowed his
coworkers to wound his spirit. Sam allowed his supervisor to determine how he would spend his time. His
employer did not respect his ability enough to compensate him financially.

God does not require that Christian men allow
everyone to run over them. Being without boundaries
is like wearing a sign that says, "Abuse me." We should
expect those at work to treat us with dignity and respect. We must defend our boundaries.

You will not protect yourself any more than you love yourself.

L. S.

> *Jesus said to him, "I do not say to you, up to seven*
> *times, but up to seventy times seven."*
>
> —MATT. 18:22

Why should I forgive her?" I cried.

Mom always became the mediator when my sister and I fought. We wanted punishment to be slow and painful while mother preferred forgiveness. She always made it sound so logical, so fair, so . . . right. Don't get me wrong, I don't mind forgiving someone, but I want to do it on my conditions. I want to get something out of the deal. Mother saw forgiving as the path to harmony; I saw it as the road to wimp city. Maybe I really was bothered because I knew I'd have to do it again sometime.

Forgiving just seems to go against our nature. Tragically, we see it as a sign of giving in.

People will fail us over and over again. That's a given. What we must realize, though, is that if we choose not to forgive, we allow bitterness and revenge to creep in. The best therapy you can give yourself is to declare forgiveness of the one that hurt you, even if this goes on for a lifetime.

Father, help me to realize that as one who was forgiven for eternity, I can surely forgive another for today.

B. D.

He will turn
The hearts of the fathers to the children,
And the hearts of the children to their fathers;
Lest I come and strike the earth with a curse.
—MAL. 4:6

I met Mike for the first time just last week. As we ate lunch together, here's the story he told me.

"You know, I'm thirty-six years old, have been a youth pastor for some time. Before that I taught high school. Most of my friends know that my dad was a drunk, that he beat us all with a belt often—and in anger. I've prayed about it and thought I'd worked through it all.

"Lately life has become, well, ordinary. I've done my job. I've prayed. But this feeling of incomplete boredom settled on me. Everything seemed so burdensome, almost lifeless.

"Then I thought of my mom and dad. Sure, I love them, but I'd never really appreciated the good things they did for me, only the bad. And I'd not told them I love them . . . so I did!"

Mike related to me the difference it had made. He was again alive, excited, appreciating his wife and kids in a new way.

Have you told your parents you love them?

Lord, help me to realize that Mom and Dad loved me the best they could.

T. S.

*For by means of a harlot
A man is reduced to a crust of bread;
And an adulteress will prey upon his
precious life.* —PROV. 6:26

I wouldn't like to be a single male today. It was hard enough being single many years ago. Nowadays a single man has an even more difficult time with his sexuality. Casual sex is glamorized through the media of television, video, magazines, and movies. For males who are uncertain about casual sex, society also offers the option of what is called safe sex.

The promise of casual sex is only an illusion, like a mirage in the desert. It temporarily anesthetizes loneliness. How is a single male to respond to the promise of casual sex?

The single male must realize the unspoken liabilities that go along with casual sex—the threat of AIDS, venereal diseases, rape accusations, and paternity suits. While it is normal to desire a woman, that sex is reserved for marriage. Exercise control over your sexual desires and focus on emotional intimacy until you marry.

Lord, help me to have control over my sexual desires.

L. S.

Counsel in the heart of man is like deep water,
But a man of understanding will draw it out.
—PROV. 20:5

Every man needs a man of understanding in his life. Men need someone who can help them see the deep needs, longings, and desires inside.

Early in my marriage I was totally frustrated with my wife over how she made pancake mix. Her resistance to doing it my way was alarming to a new groom. (I didn't even consider that she might have felt threatened by my suggestions about her cooking.) Since I wasn't getting anywhere with her, I called my friend Bill and told him about the struggle. He pointed out to me that my wife's pancake-making method was not a moral issue. There really was no right or wrong way. Bill was a friend of understanding. His counsel helped me give up a lifelong quest to make my wife make pancakes differently and to enjoy the fact that my wife makes me pancakes.

As men, we don't always see clearly the best solution to a problem on our own. Left to my own understanding, my life would have been an endless quest to make my wife make pancakes the way I believed was right. Do you have a man of understanding to discuss issues with? Are you a man of understanding to give helpful feedback to others?

Lord, help me to have the wisdom to be a man of understanding in someone's life today.

B. N.

*And Jonathan again caused David to vow, because
he loved him; for he loved him as he loved his
own soul.*
       —1 SAM. 20:17

It's been nine years since I met Hank, a recovering
drug addict and alcoholic. Like many men, he had a
problem hearing good, affirming things when they
were said to him. Low self-esteem does that to us. On
his twenty-second birthday, I sent him a card, mention-
ing some of the good things I appreciated about him. I
also told him how his friendship helped me and that I
loved him like a brother.

Several days later, Hank called me. He said, "I know
I should say thank you for the card and your kind
words, but I would appreciate you never doing anything like that again."

"Sorry, Hank," I said. "You are very important to me.
Your friendship means a great deal to me, and you'll
just have to put up with me saying good things about
you. Get used to it!"

And so he has! Eight years later, Hank is one of my
closest friends. I don't know what I would do without
him. And, believe it or not, he has become one of the
most affirming friends I have. Hank loves me . . . and I,
him.

———————

*Lord, help me to tell the Hank in my life that I care about him, that I
love him as a brother.*

            T. S.

A man who has friends must himself be friendly,
But there is a friend who sticks closer than a brother.
—PROV. 18:24

One of the most difficult pressures I have faced in my career has been having to deal with difficult people. I used to believe that if only I could get away from these people, I would be happy. This of course was impossible. There were difficult people in every department and job I went to. So I concluded that I could never work again or I could learn how to deal with them.

Difficult people are miserable inside and want everyone else to be as miserable as they are. They are insecure and compensate by controlling others. Difficult people bring out the worst in all of us; they remind us of people we have not liked before. They tell lies, gossip, and like to manipulate others.

Maybe you have to face a difficult person or persons everyday on your job. Sometimes you may dread waking up in the morning to go to work because you know they're waiting for you.

These are several ways to lighten the blow of having to work with difficult people. Don't take them personally. What they say is merely their opinion. Avoiding these people when possible is not a bad idea either. Try to be assertive, and avoid being aggressive or reactive because they can always be more so. Finally, turn to the Lord, remembering that He is the master at dealing with difficult people.

Lord, give me the strength and patience to handle difficult relationships.

L. S.

> *Those who are wise shall shine*
> *Like the brightness of the firmament,*
> *And those who turn many to righteousness*
> *Like the stars forever and ever.*
>
> —DAN. 12:3

Doing some research not long ago, I came across a stack of magazines from the late sixties and early seventies. A common theme was everyone wanting to change the world, an admirable pursuit, if you wanted to change the world for the better. And even if you could, how would you do it?

First, it would take an effective plan or course of action. This would entail knowledge and consideration. Second, it would have to have a positive outcome, and this would require positive leadership. A task with the dimensions of changing the world is not done by whim or emotion. There must be a strategy and a leader.

Even today we wish we could change the world—maybe not the whole world, but at least our small part of it. As we go through recovery we are going through change. To change our world we too must seek wisdom to keep us on target, progressing positively. We must also seek to help others. By doing so we shine as a light of change for them, an example.

Lord, grant me wisdom as I seek change in my life for the glory of God.

B. D.

You shall love your neighbor as yourself.
—MARK 12:31

Mark was young, bright, and good-looking. He was well-mannered and easygoing; but when Mark looked in the mirror, he saw a short, balding man with nothing to offer, going nowhere fast. When I told him how I saw him, he got angry, hostile, and difficult. He couldn't stand to have his negative view of himself challenged by someone else.

Does this sound familiar? Many of us struggle with the same problem: low self-esteem. Some people call it self-loathing. Whatever you call it, it does incredible damage to our relationships and our health. It can wreck our lives.

If we take Jesus seriously, we are asked to love others as we love ourselves. But we can't do it if we despise ourselves. Put another way, we can't love the Creator if we don't like the creation. Did Mark overcome his handicap? Yes! By listening to other men as they told him the truth about himself, he was slowly set free to love others and God.

Are you free to love others as you love yourself? Think about it.

_____

Dear God, please help me to see myself as You see me, through Jesus' eyes.

T. S.

> *Do not be conformed to this world, but be
> transformed by the renewing of your mind,
> that you may prove what is that good and
> acceptable and perfect will of God.*
>
> —ROM. 12:2

One strange complaint from wives in marital therapy is that their husbands spend too much time on the computer—sometimes from the time they get home from work until they go to bed.

Computers make it easy for men to work all the time. They can connect with the work computer and make business deals from the bedroom. Computers can also be used to avoid family intimacy. One computer program actually allows men to communicate with women on the screen. One man's wife divorced him when he had an affair with someone he met on the computer. In addition, computers make it easier for us not to think.

But a man can find positive uses for a computer. He can create a family budget on it. He can teach computer skills to his children; he can improve his technological skills. We must live in this rapidly changing world physically but not be caught up in it spiritually.

Lord, help me to not get caught up into the things of this world.

L. S.

They will fight against you,
But they shall not prevail against you.
For I am with you . . . to deliver you.
—JER. 1:19

My father and I had a close relationship. I was devastated when he died. If you've experienced this in your life, then you know of the emptiness one can feel. For so long I had placed so much of my dependency on my father. I guess I never entertained the prospect of his not always being around to answer my questions and even protect me from life's valleys.

At my father's passing I was a new believer. The totality of God as the heavenly Father had not really sunk in. I was still too emotionally tied to my earthly father. But there I was for the first time feeling so vulnerable and small. The man who had protected me for so long was no longer there. How would I function? How would I make it in this great big world? At that point the only thing I could think to do was open my Bible. It opened to Jeremiah, and as I began reading I came to the last part of Chapter 1. It was here that I knew that my heavenly Father was sufficient to protect and guide me through the trials of life. In my trek to adulthood I realized that when the battles of this life seem overwhelming, the Lord is there to deliver us. Jeremiah 1:18 says that God has made us as "fortified cities." Trials will come, but God is there to protect and defend.

Father, help us to know that You will deliver us.

B. D.

> *I am distressed for you, Jonathan, my brother;*
> *You were very dear to me.*
> *Your love for me was wonderful, more*
> *   wonderful than that of women.*
> —2 SAM. 1:26 NIV

Last January I spoke at two men's conferences in Canada. As I prayed over my message, a letter fell out of my Bible, a letter from Brian. After he described his recent struggles, his letter continued:

> I never intended to draw away from you. I love you and you are my dearest friend. And I had to write this to you because my greatest weakness is my inability to say it out loud. I've come way past loving you for what you've done for me. . . . It is who you are, not what you do, that makes me love you.

After I read the letter to the men, fifteen men approached me with their own stories of being unable to tell friends, parents, wives, and children of their love. Do you have someone who needs to know you love them? Maybe you should write them a letter.

Lord Jesus, help me to call or just write a note to convey my love to someone who needs to know about it today.

T. S.

*Cast your burden on the LORD,
And He shall sustain you.*
—PS. 55:22

Imagine yourself at the mouth of the Mississippi River in your swimming trunks and in great physical condition. You have trained for years under the best swimming instructors. You are in the center of the river and have been swimming upstream for a while and suddenly realize that you are extremely tired, just treading water trying to stay afloat. A boat comes by going upstream, and you grab hold of the rudder, but you can't hold on. Finally, you give up and face whatever fate the river brings you.

Trying to control your life is like trying to swim up the Mississippi. Yet a man with an addictive character believes that he can and must control his life. If he cannot control external events through manipulation, he tries to flee. Emotions are controlled via repression or aggression. If these methods don't work, he turns to an external experience or drug to numb the pain.

A master controller must relinquish domination over his internal and external world if he wants to survive. At the point of surrender in his recovery, he learns to go with life, instead of fighting it.

Recovery is living life on life's terms.

L. S.

*Again, I saw that for all toil and every skillful work
a man is envied by his neighbor. This also is vanity
and grasping for the wind.* —ECCL. 4:4

Competition and men seem to go together—in sports,
business, belongings, and so on.

Solomon reminds us that the competition can get out
of hand and become "striving after the wind." Men can
become so competitive that being the "king of the
mountain" becomes the only goal. They don't take the
time to think about what the competition is costing
them or whether they really care about the "trophy"
they're competing for.

A friend of mine spent tremendous energy to be the
best competitor in his line of business. In the process,
he lost his family, his self-respect, and finally his business.

Competition does have its positive side. Striving for
the best has produced some remarkable feats. But
competition has its downside. Strive to live a balanced
life. Don't get caught up in competition for competition's sake. Make sure it is really important to you and
doesn't interfere with other more important goals.

*Lord, help me have the wisdom to be balanced in my approach to
life.*

B. N.

Do you not know that friendship with the world is enmity with God? Whoever therefore wants to be a friend of the world makes himself an enemy of God.
—JAMES 4:4

As a young man, I was a conformist. It was very important that people like me. If people liked me, I knew I had value as a person. If they didn't, I was certain I was worthless. Most people I met in those days were, unfortunately, just like me. They valued themselves and others on externals, liking and disliking themselves and others because of appearances.

People who make judgments like that are fools. And I was the companion of fools. Eventually, through a number of painful experiences, I came into the company of wise people.

Who were these wise people? Wise people loved God and others unconditionally. They loved me for who I was. They told me the truth in love. They became God's instrument to help me change.

The wise people warmed me up with their wise counsel. Most importantly, by loving me for who I was at the time and by convincing me that they would love me no matter what, they allowed me to learn about the love of God.

Dear God, help me to forsake the company of fools, to draw my self-image from the counsel and love of Your wise people.

T. S.

> *If your right eye causes you to sin, pluck it out*
> *and cast it from you.*
> —MATT. 5:29

Pornography has zeroed in on the American male, creating what will probably be a generation of sexual addicts. Pornography is filtered right into the home through adult cable channels, magazines, video rentals, and commercial and even regular TV programming.

Pornography acts on a man's visual sexual response and his capacity to fantasize. When a male sees the body of a sexy woman, he gets aroused. The image is permanently imprinted on the mind, available for recall at any time.

Pornography diminishes sex to a raw physical experience. This is far from God's purpose for sex, which is the bonding of a male and female in a one-flesh relationship.

Looking at pornography is stimulating and supposedly fulfilling. But most sex addicts report a void or sense of guilt, followed by a need to see more.

The best way to deal with pornography is never to look at it. After all, what you have not tasted of, you cannot miss. If you have tried to stop looking at pornography and cannot, admit your powerlessness and seek help.

Lord, help me to keep my eyes on those things which are pure.

L. S.

*The thief does not come except to steal, and to kill,
and to destroy. I have come that they may have life,
and that they may have it more abundantly.*
—JOHN 10:10

Many of us remember "This Is Your Life," a TV program that saluted someone by bringing on friends and family to share the honored guest with the audience. When they brought out old friends from far in the past, I got a glimpse of what these people were like as they were younger. It was exciting to see someone successful who had enriched others' lives.

In John's gospel we are told of the abundant life Christ Jesus offers. Here are three ways to enhance our abundant life:

1. Sow for abundant life in an active response to the Great Commission. Sow the seeds of the gospel that others may obtain the abundant life.

2. Live for abundant life, acknowledging that Christian life is the best of all. This motivates us to follow Christ daily.

3. Know the source of abundant life—Jesus Christ.

Lord, thank You for new life in You. Thank You also for abundance, not of material things, but of heavenly things.

B. D.

> *A perverse man sows strife,*
> *And a whisperer separates the*
> *best of friends.*
> —PROV. 16:28

Anyone who has known me for any length of time knows that I am, or can be, difficult. Sometimes I'm insensitive, possibly even dominating. I've known about it for many years and think I've made some progress.

A personality like mine is difficult for introverted people to take on. So instead of talking to me directly, they sometimes talk to another close friend about me. By the time the message is carried, first to another friend, then to a second, and finally to me, it has changed character. It may come across more hurtfully than intended.

Okay, so what's the point? Simply put, there is no place for gossip in our relationships.

I encourage my friends to talk to me, asking for feedback. I need all the help I can get. But perhaps the best defense against gossip is communication. If I share with my friends, honestly and openly speaking the truth in love, then even a whisperer cannot separate us.

Lord, help me not to talk about other people today, but to speak the truth in love to my friends and family.

T. S.

*All things are lawful for me, but I will not be
brought under the power of any.*

—1 COR. 6:12

As John sat in my office sharing his long struggle with sexual obsession, he appeared to be defeated. John had his first experience with lust when he was twelve and encountered one of his older sister's girlfriends unclad. John was ashamed. He knew that the feelings he experienced were wrong. This was the beginning of John's thirty-year struggle with lust. John undressed thousands of women in his mind—even close female friends and family members.

As a Christian John felt that God would not hear him until he gave up his lust. This was John's biggest mistake—alienating himself to stand alone against a power that would soon be greater than he. It is important to realize that God knows our every thought and fantasy. It does no good to try to hide from God, and He will help us. God wants us to admit our sexual trials and come to Him daily as He equips us to fight the battle.

When we admit to God that we are weak we become strong.

L. S.

> *There is one alone, without companion:*
> *He has neither son nor brother.*
> *Yet there is no end to all his labors.*
> *Nor is his eye satisfied with riches.*
> *But he never asks,*
> *"For whom do I toil and deprive*
> *myself of good?"*
> —ECCL. 4:8

Single men need to think about these words of wisdom from Solomon. Singleness has many advantages and disadvantages. We need to have purpose in our life, and this purpose must go beyond ourselves.

If we set our eyes on God, He can direct our life goals. I worked with a single man who had been successful in business and had all the material blessings a person could want. He finally realized he did not have a cause greater than himself. As we discussed the true meaning in life, he recognized he had not been living for God. His commitment to God's purposes for his life brought him peace.

Do you have a greater purpose than yourself as you live your life? We all need to think about this whether we are married or single.

Lord, help me to see beyond today and to place You at the center of my priorities.

B. N.

Greater love has no one than this, than to lay down one's life for his friends. —JOHN 15:13

I heard this verse when I was a little boy in Sunday school. It impressed me then as very heroic. You know, like taking the bullet meant for your buddy during the war or volunteering for medical research or being like Jesus and dying for others. Yes, I thought it was sacrificial and heroic, and I was right, but not for the reasons I thought.

My Sunday school teacher back then was Mr. Johnston, a middle-aged, hardworking man with a potbelly and thinning hair who taught junior-high-aged children about the Bible and about Jesus. He was there every Sunday (I was not), patiently teaching the lesson, despite our early teen antics. You know what? Mr. Johnston laid down his life for us.

Mr. Johnston gave of himself to me, gave himself up so that thirty years later I remember him and what he taught me. He has been dead now for many years, but I look forward to seeing him again, just to say "Thanks."

Lord, help me to appreciate those who lay down their lives for me today and to lay down my life for them.

T. S.

> *The Lord does not see as man sees; for man looks at the outward appearance, but the Lord looks at the heart.*
> —1 SAM. 16:7

Maybe when you graduated from high school, you did not need more education to get your job. Now years later one might need a college degree and certification to get your job. It can be frightening to work around men who are younger and more educated than you are. Maybe your employer has hinted that you should go back to school. Seeing younger men promoted over you can also make you feel that you're not educated enough.

A lot can be said for education. I know—I've been in school for fifteen years since high school. But probably more can be said about experience. When I finished graduate school in psychology, I had a lot of knowledge but no experience. I felt like an educated incompetent. Although my education was helpful, my experience taught me how to do my job.

If you feel undereducated, don't lose hope or confidence. Your experience is priceless. You might have to update your knowledge now and then, but there is no better teacher than the real thing.

An educated man has knowledge but he may not have wisdom.

L. S.

*For whatever is born of God overcomes the world.
And this is the victory that has overcome the
world—our faith.*   —1 JOHN 5:4

I admire triathletes. They get their kicks spending a
day swimming, biking, and running incredible dis-
tances. I competed in a triathlon a few years ago to
see what it would be like. It was a sprint triathlon—
everything was cut down to a distance suitable to mere
mortals.

I trained hard but truly tested my mettle in the ac-
tual events. None of the events individually seemed too
difficult, but putting them all together was more than I
expected.

I swam in a flurry of energy. During the biking I felt
myself slowing a bit. By the middle of the running, I
was questioning my sanity. Somehow I began questioning myself more, feeling all alone on the course.
How would I finish? Would I finish? I needed something—something to push me to the finish line. I remembered my wife assuring me that she would see me
at the finish line. Wow! *That's it,* I thought. *She's there
waiting for me. I can't give up.*

Life is just like this. Some situations make us think
about giving up, but if we remember God is waiting for
us at the finish line, we keep moving forward.

Lord, give me endurance to continue in life's race.

B. D.

*You are My friends if you do whatever I
command you.*
—JOHN 15:14

As I write this, I am coming out of a bad time in my
life. I have burned out! That's right, I have gotten the
complaint common to many in ministry—I'm out of
gas! How did it happen? There are many contributing
factors, but I'll write only about one here: disobedience. I have been disobedient without knowing it.

My ministry, my calling if you will, is the delight of
my heart. God has uniquely prepared me for it, and I
am truly grateful. But somewhere along the way I began to sacrifice rather than obey. I worked long into
the night, instead of obeying God's command to live a
balanced life. I overcommitted myself, thinking only I
could perform certain tasks, although the Lord wanted
me to depend on and strengthen my brothers and sisters. I was arrogant where He would have me humble,
brash where He would have me gentle, and depending
upon myself rather than on Him.

I wish to be God's friend, to be in harmony with His
plan for my life, to be a good team player. And He's
given me another chance to do just that. I'm very
grateful and hope I can remember this lesson: "To
obey is better than sacrifice" (1 Sam. 15:22).

*Lord, please show me today how I can best play on Your team. Please
teach me obedience.*

T. S.

I beseech you therefore, brethren, by the mercies of God, that you present your bodies a living sacrifice, holy, acceptable to God, which is your reasonable service.
—ROM. 12:1

Recall a possession of great value to you, either material or sentimental. It could be an heirloom, a collector's item, jewelry, or even an automobile. You probably take special care to see that no one steals it, and you make sure that it remains untouched or untarnished. If anything happened to it, you would probably be angry or upset. Now recall a possession of no value to you. Think about how you care for it and how you let others treat it. You treat something of value much differently from something of no value.

Valuing oneself is one of the most important elements of successful recovery. A man will only preserve and protect himself to the extent that he perceives his personal value. Most alcoholics would not pour alcohol over their sports cars, but freely pour alcohol into their tender bodies.

A man has to love and respect himself to be able to say no to his addiction. Those who do not value themselves will continue to behave self-destructively.

Lord, help me to remember that my body is a temple wherein the Holy Spirit lives.

L. S.

> *As he came from his mother's womb, naked*
>   *shall he return,*
> *To go as he came;*
> *And he shall take nothing from his labor*
> *Which he may carry away in his hand.*
>   —ECCL. 5:15

Someone once pointed out that we never see a U-Haul™ behind a hearse. Solomon reflects on this truth as he states that when we enter this world we bring nothing but our bodies and that it will be the same when we leave.

Two things will last eternally. They are the souls of men and the Word of God.

Many men have committed themselves to the purposes of God. A friend of mine, Ken Canfield, executive director of the National Center for Fathering, has committed himself to strengthening the role of the father. He sees the need to support and encourage fathers in their important role. The lives that are affected by the work he does is an eternal investment.

What eternal impact are you having in your world? You may be making million-dollar deals in your business or constructing beautiful homes for others. Although the job you do is essential to your survival, none of it will last forever, except your influence on the souls of other people and the time you spend learning the Word of God.

Lord, help me to develop a plan of action to have an eternal impact on my world.

                                        B. N.

*Made a searching and fearless moral inventory
of ourselves.*
—THE TWELVE STEPS OF ALCOHOLICS ANONYMOUS

*Therefore take heed that the light which is in you is
not darkness.*   —LUKE 11:35

Just one week sober, still sick and shaking, I read the Twelve Steps for the first time. The fourth step was especially frightening. My whole life was a lie—to everyone, especially myself. I couldn't tell the difference between truth and a lie.

I was desperate. I knew I would die if I ever drank again. Still, the thought of putting everything objectionable about myself on paper was terrifying. I was told simply to do my best.

My best at that time was not very good. As I reread that first fourth step today, I noticed that my fear still caused me to lie.

As time went on, I wrote thirteen more fourth steps, each one more accurate that the one before. Slowly I realized that we all struggle with character defects. I learned to patiently check the light within and accept and expect progress rather than perfection.

God, give me strength as I continue to take personal inventory. Show me the truth so that I can be sure that the light within is not darkness.

T. S.

> *Examine yourselves as to whether you are in the faith. Prove yourselves. Do you not know yourselves, that Jesus Christ is in you?*
> —2 COR. 13:5

Personality is dynamic because it changes and grows constantly. One is born with a temperament. But personality is the way in which a man experiences, perceives, relates to, and responds to the happenings of his life. A man does have a choice in the matter of his personality.

The Twelve Steps point out that an addict possesses certain personality or character defects, which are to be monitored and removed on a daily basis: control, impatience, intolerance, procrastination, jealousy, manipulation, isolation, perfectionism, and many others. A man in recovery must deal with the defects in his personality daily because his personality determines his response to his world. If a man is intolerant and perfectionistic, he is likely to be angry and frustrated all the time. Being angry and frustrated can turn into an excuse to drink for tension relief.

The daily inventory provides for the adjustment of a man's personality. If a man prays for the mind of Christ daily and monitors himself honestly, making necessary personality changes, he can have a positive recovery process.

Lord, I pray that my personality will be a reflection of You.

L. S.

Though an army should encamp
against me,
My heart shall not fear.
—PS. 27:3

Like many, I believed that when I grew up I wouldn't be afraid of anything. Shadows don't scare me now, nor do trees brushing against the house, but I do still get scared.

For most kids fear comes out at night, in the dark when things aren't so easily seen. This is the same way it happens to me today. Working hard and having so many responsibilities can be intimidating. After a long day I'm ready for sleep. What I find myself doing, though, is thinking about all the "scary" things that can happen to me. When things are quiet my thoughts become louder and fears become bigger. It would be so easy if I could crawl into bed with Daddy. He would protect me.

The great news is that we can run to our heavenly Father for protection. When the fears and stresses of life seem to be waiting under your bed, rest assured that God the Father is there to help you. The best way to overcome your fear is to acknowledge it and then take it to the Father. Let Him get rid of the shadows and quiet the trees.

Heavenly Father, I have fears like a child. Help me to realize my comfort is in You.

B. D.

> *For there is nothing covered that will not be*
> *revealed, nor hidden that will not be known.*
> —LUKE 12:2

Everyone I have ever met in Twelve-Step programs confesses discomfort and fear about doing the fourth step. This is true even when people have been at it for many years. There is something quite intimidating about taking your own moral temperature. Still, we must do it or die, either physically or spiritually.

My friend Frank uses a little trick to make doing this step easier: He says, "It's inevitable!" And that is what the Scripture says. Eventually all that we have tried so hard to conceal will be revealed. Since it's inevitable, we should welcome the opportunity to confess our misdemeanors, to gain the peace and serenity of a clear conscience.

I'm no fool. I know Frank's trick is a gimmick, but so what? Be encouraged! God wants you to clear away the wreckage of the past and join us in seeking a useful life with a clear conscience.

God, please help me to continue my personal inventory. Help me to face the fear, knowing You will make all things right.

T. S.

Be anxious for nothing, but in everything by prayer and supplication, with thanksgiving, let your requests be made known to God. —PHIL. 4:6

At some point you have been told not to worry. If you are human, those words probably got no further than your ears.

Steve worried day and night. He worried about getting to work on time, how his boss was going to treat him, and whether he was going to make enough money for the month. Steve worried about whether his wife really loved him and if she saw other men as better than him.

It is almost natural for a man to worry about his job, family, and finances. But it is unnatural for a man's worries to affect his job, family, and finances adversely.

A man can worry less if he channels his energy into actions to solve problems. Remember that man cannot accurately predict or control encounters in his life.

When a man worries he does not completely trust God's sovereignty.

L. S.

> *All the labor of man is for his mouth,*
> *And yet the soul is not satisfied.*
> —ECCL. 6:7

Hunger is an interesting physical drive. It functions like the warning light on the dashboard of an automobile to inform us that something needs attention in our bodies.

Man's work is an attempt to fill an emptiness or hunger in his life. We work to have bread to eat and shelter. But work doesn't meet all of man's needs. No matter how much a person accomplishes, how much he earns, his soul is still not satisfied. Financial success is not the answer to life's problems. Man has a spiritual need that can only be filled by God.

My dad has often given the advice that the world has a lot to offer, but only God can make the "true" difference in my life. If I keep looking to my job, my wife, my family, or my things to fulfill me, I will always be hungry for more.

—————

God, help to satisfy my hunger in life by filling my life with Yours.

B. N.

Take heed and beware of covetousness, for one's life does not consist in the abundance of the things he possesses.   —LUKE 12:15

My friend Mitchell died last year. He was thirty-nine years old and in good health when he died suddenly of a heart attack. We were great friends, Mitch and I, and I have missed him every day since his death.

While he was well educated, achieving his master's degree in business administration shortly before his death, he joked about his tee-shirt, which said, "No MBA, No BMW, no Condo." Mitch hated materialism. The notion commonly held today, even among Christians, that the one who dies with the most toys wins, made us both cringe. And when Mitch died, he left behind every material possession he ever had. He left this world as he came in: with nothing but his soul.

"Take heed," for your life does not consist of what you possess.

Lord, help me to see my possessions as things You have provided for my use and pleasure. Help me today to value people and life above all other things.

T. S.

But I do not want you to be ignorant . . .
concerning those who have fallen asleep, lest you
sorrow as others who have no hope.
—1 THESS. 4:13

Sam was forty when he first came for help at the addictions recovery unit. Sam had started drinking when he was twenty-five. Before then he had never touched a drink. Al, who was also in his forties when he first came for help started drinking at thirty. Bill started drinking when he was twenty-seven.

What do Sam, Al, and Bill have in common? They all started drinking as adults, and then all suffered traumatic losses around the time they started drinking. Sam's wife committed suicide; a drunk driver killed Al's wife and daughter; and Bill's father died in a construction accident.

Sam, Al, and Bill were unable to handle loss. They also felt responsible for the death of the loved one. The alcohol anesthetized them and punished them as they felt they deserved.

To find recovery these men had to accept their losses; process the emotional pain; face their use of alcohol to maintain their avoidance; and give up their false guilt.

———————

Because of Christ, you may see your loved one on the other side.

L. S.

. . . through faith and patience inherit the promises.
—HEB. 6:12

By nature I want everything "yesterday." Whether it's dinner or a movie, a plane or an appointment, I don't like waiting. You'd think that as much traveling as I do and as many delays as I find in airports, I would get over this. I wish I could say that I have.

As luck usually has it, I am taken through my paces when I'm really trying to control my impatience. Invariably as I am trying to make an appointment I try the newest shortcut that turns into a nightmare or I can't seem to communicate with someone over the phone. The longer that I allow this to affect me, the harder I find it to experience the other fruits of the Spirit. Moreover, my witness for Christ may be hindered.

We all need patience, and we need it now! And we find it in the same place that we find peace and gentleness—the Holy Spirit. In Him we find comfort, understanding, and perspective—a perspective that puts all the miscommunication, delays, and urgency in their proper place—a jar labeled Unimportant.

Father, give me a proper perspective in daily activity. Help me to be patient that others may see a glimpse of You.

B. D.

> *Take heed to yourselves. If your brother sins against*
> *you, rebuke him; and if he repents, forgive him.*
> —LUKE 17:3

Resentment is the number one offender." So says the Big Book of AA. The unwillingness to forgive is at the heart of many a tormented man.

Perhaps, as this verse suggests, our inability to rebuke or confront our brothers contributes to our inability to forgive them.

Scott is a friend of long standing. He and I have had many adventures together since we joined AA. Then something almost ruined our friendship. When Scott got married, he sent me an invitation. I was going to be out of town on business that weekend, but I forgot to RSVP. After his honeymoon Scott asked me out for coffee and confronted me. I told him I was sorry, and he forgave me.

Such seemingly small things often are not done because of hurt, pride, or fear. And great relationships are destroyed over trivial matters.

Can we learn to rebuke one another so that we may forgive each other?

Father, help me to see where I need to confront someone I love today, to forgive him and cleanse my heart of bitterness.

T. S.

Pursue peace with all men, and holiness, without which no one will see the Lord. —HEB. 12:14

Steps 8 and 9 of the Twelve Steps are about the need to make amends to those individuals who have been harmed as a result of one's addiction. Every man who wishes to obtain the rewards of true recovery must walk through the valley of amends—but later rather than sooner. I recommend waiting six months to one year before making certain amends.

Many men in early recovery get excited about going out and apologizing to everyone that they've offended. But Step 9 warns a man not to make an amends if it would hurt rather than help someone. In some cases the hurt is so deep that the best amends a man could make would be never to see or talk to the hurt individual again.

Before making an amends it is important to establish a history of recovery. Over time family and friends usually lose respect and trust for the addict, so it isn't realistic to expect that everyone will trust your announcement that you're in recovery and you're sorry. If your amends is backed up by a history of healthy and responsible behavior, the person may believe what you say and forgive from the heart.

Lord, show me when and with whom I am ready to make an amends.

L. S.

> *Do not hasten in your spirit to be angry,*
> *For anger rests in the bosom of fools.*
> —ECCL. 7:9

Most men struggle to express tenderness, fear, hurt, sadness. Many men don't have any trouble expressing their anger, most of the time in destructive ways.

Anger is a strong emotion. It results in physical changes such as flushed face, increased heart rate and blood pressure, and a rush of adrenaline. When it is expressed negatively, it can do a great deal of damage.

In counseling I have worked with many men who told of the impact an angry father has had on them. Anger can leave many scars deep in the human soul. I saw this myself with my own daughter. I disciplined her in anger. Several weeks later she asked me why I was so angry with her and went on to describe the day we both remembered. It forced me to realize how much my anger towards my daughter affects her. I know I'll never be a perfect father, but I want to be more aware of how I express anger with my daughter and with other people.

We need to be slow to anger and to see that anger can be very destructive.

Lord, melt the anger in my heart with the warmth of Your love.

B. N.

*For what I am doing, I do not understand. For
what I will to do, that I do not practice; but what
I hate, that I do.* —ROM. 7:15

All my life I struggled with guilt; I always felt that I
was a bad person, weak-willed, letting God down. I
really wanted to be better, but like Paul, I ended up
doing what I should not. I thought I was the only one
who did that. I still believed that church was filled with
perfect people and that I just couldn't measure up. The
harder I tried, the worse it was.

Nothing changed when I arrived in AA. I was still
different, still the odd man out. I was bad when others
were good. Of course others should get well. They deserved it, but not me! I was unique, terminally unique.

The fourth step began the process of change. Very
slowly, as I listened, as I learned, I found that the people in church really weren't perfect, just forgiven. We
were all sinners in need of a Savior. We all needed
God's grace every day, just as Paul did.

*God, thank You for the honesty of Paul, telling me that I am not
unique. I pray that You will use me to set others free from terminal
uniqueness.*

T. S.

> *For let not that man suppose that he will receive*
> *anything from the Lord; he is a double-minded*
> *man, unstable in all his ways.* —JAMES 1:7–8

When Don entered treatment, he said, "I drink alcohol, spend a lot of money, and do some marijuana; but I only have a problem with alcohol." He believed he could quit drinking and continue his compulsive spending and marijuana use. Don was bargaining, giving up one addiction while at the same time maintaining another or picking up a more applauded or acceptable one.

Bargaining is like trying to change cabins on the *Titanic*. The ship is going to sink, but a few believe up to the last moment that they can avoid the inevitable by running to the other end of the ship.

Bargaining often goes unnoticed and unaddressed because it gives the illusion that one has actually given up his addiction. True recovery requires total abstinence in both of a man's primary and secondary addictions. When a man bargains, he only postpones his honest entry into recovery.

There is no room for dishonesty in recovery.

L. S.

These things I have written to you who believe in the name of the Son of God, that you may know that you have eternal life.   —1 JOHN 5:13

Beyond any reasonable doubt." This phrase is used in courts across the land. The decision made by the jury is based on hearing and believing (or not believing) what has been presented. Either way it is crucial that they come to a decision and stand by it, never wavering, never a doubt. It is here, at this point, that the jurors may say that they are assured of the conclusion.

In our Christian walk we are attacked by Satan. One of his greatest weapons is doubt. Doubt is that shady character that seeks to complicate what we have heard and what we believe, so we may need to reevaluate the evidence just as we must evaluate testimony in a court of law. The testimony that is most powerful is that of God's Word—God's truth. As we stand before our accuser, we can stand confident and convinced of the reality of God's work through Jesus Christ. Here lies the evidence: We were once condemned, but by the grace and love of God the Father, we were released from our sentence and given a new identity. We now stand cleared and forgiven for eternity—acquitted.

There is no one or nothing that can take away this pardon, this freedom.

Lord, I acknowledge You as Lord and Savior. By grace I am free.

B. D.

> *Let us walk properly, as in the day, not in revelry*
> *and drunkenness, not in licentiousness and*
> *lewdness, not in strife and envy. But put on the*
> *Lord Jesus Christ, and make no provision for the*
> *flesh, to fulfill its lust.* —ROM. 13:13–14

Have you ever asked the purpose of the fourth step? Why is it necessary to dredge up the past?

I prefer to be up and about in the daytime. When I've worked at night, I've realized that something is out of synch. Sin is like that for me. When I do day work, I seek to live honestly, uprightly before God. When I do night work, I seek to fulfill my lust.

My employment application for day work is the fourth step. Here I list my qualifications for day work (positive character traits) as well as the reasons I should not work at night (my character defects). I have come to appreciate day work because it gives me a life in balance, where vision is as far as the horizon, not obscured by darkness. Doing day work allows me to be in synch with God and my fellow man.

God, help me to use the fourth step to apply for day work. Let the misdeeds of the past press me on to live in the light with You.

T. S.

Forsake foolishness and live,
And go in the way of understanding.
—PROV. 9:6

Matthew's closest friends, physician, pastor, employer, and family tried to convince him that he needed help for his alcohol addiction. They told him how he had hurt them and that he was destroying his own life. Matthew just shook his head and said, "I realize how each of you feels, and I do appreciate your concern; but I really feel I have my drinking under control." Matthew later went through a treatment program because his wife threatened to leave him. To my knowledge, he never recovered.

There was no way that Matthew could have recovered. He had not bottomed out, so he didn't realize what a serious problem he really had.

Bottoming out is like falling out of an airplane with a parachute that won't open. The man who is falling knows he has a problem, but doesn't realize how bad it is till he hits the bottom. Had Matthew bottomed out, he might have realized *how bad* things really were.

A man does not have to hit bottom and lose everything. The choice for recovery can be made at any point.

_____

If you put off getting help till you hit bottom, it may be too late.

L. S.

> *For there is not a just man on*
> *earth who does good*
> *And does not sin.*
> —ECCL. 7:20

Larry was obsessed with doing things the right way. He felt as if he could never make a mistake. But, of course, this is impossible; so inevitably he failed at his quest. He came to counseling and discovered that deep down he felt unlovable and thought that the only way God would accept him was if he were perfect.

Perfectionism is a problem that strikes many people. Men have a need to be perfect to cover up their fear of inadequacy. The Bible states that "all have sinned and fall short of the glory of God" (Rom. 3:23). Solomon reminds us, too, that indeed we are not perfect. The only perfect person who ever lived was Jesus Christ. We, too, can enjoy the fellowship with a perfect God by acknowledging that we have sinned and need Jesus Christ as our Savior and Lord.

Help me to see that God is the only perfect One and that I can enjoy fellowship with Him through a relationship with Jesus Christ.

B. N.

*For we dare not class ourselves or compare
ourselves with those who commend themselves.
But they, measuring themselves by themselves, and
comparing themselves among themselves, are
not wise.*   —2 COR. 10:12

I was once a follower of the "Don't make waves, I'm okay, you're okay" school. The idea is that we compare ourselves to some dreadful person such as Idi Amin or Adolph Hitler, which leaves us, we think, looking pretty good; after all, we haven't killed six million Jews or murdered in the middle of the night. We're okay, right?

Wrong! I remember that as I explained to my sponsor that I felt guilty about some of my past conduct, he told me, "You shouldn't just feel guilty—you are guilty!" The things I had done were wrong. I had hurt innocent people, most often by using their love for me to get what I wanted. I was not okay, but beginning with the honest inventory of the fourth step I could enter a process to be okay.

So I took an honest look. And by God's grace, one day at a time, I am okay. Jesus died so that I could be okay.

Lord, thank You for sending honest people into my life to show me the way out. Help me to compare myself to Your Son Jesus rather than to the people around me.

                                                    T. S.

> *Commit your works to the LORD,*
> *And your thoughts will be established.*
> —PROV 16:3

Choosing the right career is like being lost in a forest and having to choose a road out. Some men, however, never choose a road, or they continually go down the same dead-end roads. Where are you in your career?

To choose the right career, you need realistic and obtainable goals. If you're forty-five and have never boxed in your life, you're not likely to become a world class boxer. Also consider your personality. If you're impatient, you probably don't need to go into teaching.

Look also at your physical and mental capabilities. Some men are cut out for hard physical labor, and some aren't. A right-brain person would probably do well at a creative profession. A left-brained man would likely enjoy engineering or accounting.

Finally, a Christian man must consider God's will and plan for his life. Through prayer, an open mind, patience, and a willing heart, along with the practical considerations, God's will for you can be revealed.

———————

You will never find peace at work until you're doing what God really wants you to do.

L. S.

If your sons will keep My covenant
And My testimony which I shall teach them,
Their sons also shall sit upon your throne
    forevermore.   **—PS. 132:12**

As men we are responsible for passing on the family name. Generation to generation the name goes on. We also pass on to our children who we are and how we act. Fathers can shape and mold a child's view of the world and others in it. As adults we must not shirk this tremendous responsibility. We see much of what we have learned from our fathers in ourselves. Invariably those things will be passed through us to our kids.

As children of God we have been given a legacy of love, a legacy of hope for eternity, a legacy steeped in the Cross. God the Father wants us all to pass this legacy down to our children that they may experience the joy of living in the family of God.

What kind of legacy are you leaving your children? Will your generation of children realize the love that is theirs through Christ Jesus or will they only receive a name?

————————

Lord, as You transcend generations help me to leave my children, as well as the people I come in contact with, the legacy of salvation.

                                   B. D.

> *Examine yourselves as to whether you are in the faith. Prove yourselves. Do you not know yourselves, that Jesus Christ is in you?*
> —2 COR. 13:5

Any moral inventory includes spiritual examination. Exactly where are we in our relationship to God? Here we will need the help of an understanding friend or mentor. In AA we call such a man a sponsor.

As a Christian man in recovery, you must find another Christian man to help you spiritually. He will need to have traveled your path and been where you have been, to be someone in whom you have confidence, faith, and trust. He will need to be able to provide counsel as you look at your prayer, meditation, Bible study, and worship. The importance of such a sponsor cannot be overstated. Going it alone spiritually is dangerous.

When you have found such a friend, you will find ways to be helpful to him. Every Christian needs opportunity to help someone else along.

As you approach a searching spiritual inventory, find a sponsor, a mentor, a friend. You will both benefit.

Dear God, as I grow, convince me of my need for the help of an understanding friend. Please provide that sponsor for me.

T. S.

*Let your conduct be without covetousness, and
be content with such things as you have. For
He Himself said, "I will never leave you nor
forsake you."*
—HEB. 13:5

Allan was not satisfied with life. In fifteen years he went through two wives, twelve cars, seven boats, and over twenty hobbies. He tried mountain climbing, speedboat racing, car and gun collecting, cliff skiing, and kickboxing. Allan also moved five times, lost three homes, lost thousands of dollars in investments, and started several businesses. Unfortunately, Allan's fifteen-year search for fulfillment through variety and materialism led him nowhere.

One character defect found in the addictive personality is compulsiveness. The compulsive person is driven to repeat certain behaviors and is inclined to seek out pleasurable experiences or sensations.

The recovery entails learning to be satisfied, to internalize contentment. In recovery one learns to appreciate nature, walks in the park, and moments of solitude. At last there can actually be a point of enough.

Lord, create in me a peaceful and contented spirit.

L. S.

> *If the ax is dull,*
> *And one does not sharpen the edge,*
> *Then he must use more strength;*
> *But wisdom brings success.*
> —ECCL. 10:10

When we try to make life work with our dull, foolish minds, we use up more strength and get less satisfying results. When we turn to God and ask for His wisdom, we can know true success without wasting energy.

As a young teenager I asked for wisdom. I claimed James 1:5: "If any of you lacks wisdom, let him ask of God, who gives to all liberally and without reproach, and it will be given to him." I asked God for wisdom about girls, parties, and so on. Through life I have continued to do this.

When I have not asked for His wisdom and thought I could do it better myself, I used much more effort. I was changing the sparkplugs in my wife's car one day. I changed every one of them with ease, a task I felt well-equipped to do. But I couldn't get the last one out. I spent two hours in the freezing weather looking for a way to get that sparkplug out so I could replace it. Finally, I just said, "God, please show me how I can get this plug out." I reached down, and it came out in my hand. God lovingly continues to remind me that He is the true source of wisdom.

Father, sharpen my mind with godly wisdom for today.

B. N.

But let each one examine his own work, and then
he will have rejoicing in himself alone, and not
in another. —GAL. 6:4

Once a year, near the time of my birthday, I take a weekend to myself for reflection and prayer. I do this at a Jesuit retreat house where the retreats are silent. From Friday evening until Sunday afternoon, we do not speak.

I find it necessary to draw alone into myself with the Lord only, being quiet so that He can speak to me through His Word, through the retreat master, and through my own meditation. I always bring along paper and pencil and write new insights into myself: my depravity, my willfulness as well as my desire to know and to love God more fully. I will share this inventory with my friends at a later time, but for now it is just to assist me as I look into myself at a time of reflection.

My sponsor taught me to do this, and I would like to do the same for you. Please take time to be alone with the Lord in a private place. I guarantee a positive result.

Lord God, thank You for a time of quiet reflection with You. I pray
You will provide those times for me to see deep within myself, with
Your help.

T. S.

*A man shall leave his father and mother and be
joined to his wife, and they shall become one flesh.*
—GEN. 2:24

A single male can find it difficult to achieve physical and emotional separation from his parents. If his dependency needs were not met early in life, he may have difficulty leaving home. If he was overprotected, he may also fear leaving the nest.

Emotional incest between a mother and her son can keep an adult male from breaking the emotional and physical ties. He feels guilty about abandoning Mom, who plays the role of a surrogate wife, so he cannot have his own life. He may even feel he must remain dependent until his mom and dad can reconnect.

Failure to separate from Mom can hinder male development. It can keep a man from marrying at the right time and can retard his intellectual, spiritual, and social development. It may even limit his vocational advancement.

To cut loose a man must admit that he is in an unhealthy relationship with his mom. Then he must be willing to begin the separation process, knowing that someone's feelings will be hurt. Finally, he must set boundaries to protect the new relationship.

Separating from parents is just a new dimension of the relationship.

L. S.

Then He said to His disciples, "The harvest truly is plentiful, but the laborers are few."
—MATT. 9:37

I heard a story of a city kid visiting his uncle's farm. Extremely early the first morning he was roused out of bed by a cousin and led around the farm doing everything from feeding the chickens to milking the cows— all before the sun was actually visible. Upon completing those tasks the city boy and his cousin went into the house for breakfast. After being satisfied by ham, eggs, and biscuits the city boy excused himself from the table and started back to bed. He had gotten only two steps away when his uncle asked what he was doing. After telling the uncle of his plan to slumber, he was rudely awakened. The uncle informed him that there was work to do. The boy wondered how this could be as he explained all that he had done. The uncle replied, "Those, my son, were chores. The real work is out in the fields."

And so it is in the Christian life. We too have chores. Reading Scripture, praying, tithing, and fellowshipping are just a few. These are the things that build up the church as well as ourselves. The work, however, is still in the fields. The work we are called to do, the work of the Great Commission, can be long and tedious, and it must be approached with care.

Lord, may I never grow tired of serving You and may I always be aware of the work in the field.

B. D.

If anyone will not work, neither shall he eat.
—2 THESS. 3:10

Have you noticed something about young people today? They seem to be hung up on security. It is so obvious: get a good job, get an MBA, get a big house, and so on, that I wonder if our generation has done something wrong!

What is the purpose of our work? The world seems to say that we work so that we can have things in great abundance. Yet the Scripture says that work is connected to physical sustenance. If I look at work as something to keep me going for God's work, then my focus is outward, on others. If I look upon work as something to gratify my wants, then the focus is inward, on my own comfort.

As men in recovery, we are aware that selfishness, self-centeredness is the root of all our problems. We therefore need to view our work as pleasing to God, providing sustenance for us as we seek to do His will, not a gratification of our own desires.

Why are you going to work today?

Lord, let me see work as an opportunity to serve You and know You better. Keep my focus outward, on You and my fellows.

T. S.

He who is slothful in his work
Is a brother to him who is a
great destroyer.
—PROV. 18:9

If we took an inventory of how much time we waste each day, we would probably be surprised. Yet we claim that we don't have enough time to do what we need to do. We believe that God should have given us thirty-six hours in a day. Jesus appeared to have all the time He needed to accomplish His tasks. If He has called you to a task, then you can be sure that He has given you a sufficient amount of time to complete the task. You may just not be a good steward of your time.

You can improve your efficiency. Find out what monopolizes your time. Is it people-pleasing activity, television, naps, disorganization, poor travel decisions, the phone, or worry? Then cut down on the hours you work to leave you with more energy when you do work. Finally, delegate, learn to say no, refuse to procrastinate, keep on a schedule, and prioritize your daily activities. As your efficiency rises, so should your attitude, energy, and happiness.

The man who controls his time can accomplish much.

L. S.

Let us hear the conclusion of the whole matter:
"Fear God and keep His commandments,
For this is the whole duty of man."
—ECCL. 12:13

Who had the highest IQ? According to the Bible, Solomon was the wisest man who ever lived. Of course, that he had the highest IQ could never be validated. However, it is worth heeding the wisdom of a man who asked God to give him wisdom. Ecclesiastes is a record of his search for happiness. He concluded his search with the words of today's Scriptures. Fear God and keep His commandments.

God has given us a simple plan to make this life work. First, we need to respect God. This means giving Him the honor and glory He so justly deserves. Second, we are to obey God's Word.

One of my friends who was a theologian studied God's Word all of his adult life. He died recently. Shortly before he died, I spent some time with him. He shared how the Lord had been preparing him for his own death. He talked about the deep conversations he had with his loving Father. He truly practiced the suggestion made by Solomon. It didn't make him the richest man, nor even the best-known theologian. It made him a friend of God.

Give me strength to follow Your plan for my life.

B. N.

*God is not unjust to forget your work and labor of
love which you have shown toward His name, in
that you have ministered to the saints, and do
minister.*
—HEB. 6:10

Right now I'm very tired. I have written fifteen of
these devotionals today. I've worked hard all day. And
as I write I'm holding on to Paul's promise that God
remembers our work as we minister to the saints. I
really hope God remembers this day.

Do you get tired in your personal ministry? It may
be church committees or youth work, lifestyle evange-
lism, or being a good husband and father. Whatever it
is, we all get tired. And we need to remember that God
does not forget our work in ministry. He honors it, just
as we honor Him by performing it.

If you feel you have no ministry, think again! Any
Christian man is hard put not to have a ministry. Even
a kind word, a cup of cold water, a simple kindness
such as holding a door open for a stranger, all these
things are ministry in Jesus' behalf. So as I bring my
day to a close, I rest in the assurance that God remembers this work. And He remembers yours as well!

*God, thank You for remembering my toil today. Thank You for allow-
ing me the privilege of ministering in Your name.*

T. S.

> *Why should you, my son, be enraptured*
> *by an immoral woman,*
> *And be embraced in the arms of a seductress?*
> —PROV. 5:20

You have worked all day long. Your boss praises you and single women in the office flatter you. On the way home you anticipate your wife's praise for your achievements. To your disillusionment, your wife doesn't even greet you at the door. In fact, she appears irritated with you and wants to talk about how you never help her around the house. You, of course, are very wounded inside.

This so-called pedestal syndrome is common for men. We are like gods at work, and when we come home we are brought back down to earth.

A danger of this syndrome is its tendency to lead a man to seek more female affirmation at work by flirting, exchanging sexual innuendoes with female peers, seduction, and even a literal affair.

Remember that we are never complete without oneness with our wives. The flattery of the single women at work may be a temporary fix, but only leads to more sexual vulnerability. We must uplift our wives. Then, they may feel more like affirming us.

Lord, help me to turn to Your gift for my completeness.

L. S.

We who first trusted in Christ should be to the praise of His glory.
—EPH. 1:12

What's this Christian stuff all about?" I was taken back by the bluntness of the question. As I scrambled to compose and gather my thoughts, the inquisitor sat back as if to say, "Take your time. I'm not going anywhere."

The simplest thing I could come up with was "Living for Christ." This was also the safest, or so I thought.

"What does that entail?" This was not getting any easier. I figured the best thing to do would be to take a breath, relax, and say a quick prayer. As I dove in I realized my perspective was clearing. This Christian "stuff" was in fact all about living for Christ. There are many things to follow or agree with, but there is only one thing to live for. The believer makes a choice to follow Christ totally or cast Him to the wind like so many other "reasons" for living.

When we evaluate our lives, what do we see as our passion? Is it the search for wealth, the acquiring of power, or that God may be glorified? We should aspire for the latter. To live for something suggests that our life's motivation centers around it. Everything else pales in comparison to its place in our lives. This is no more true than in the Christian life. Our motivation is the Cross. Our purpose is to glorify God. What are you living for? A fading possession or an eternal Savior?

Lord, help me to recognize You as my purpose in life.

B. D.

> *Six days you shall do your work, and on the*
> *seventh day you shall rest.*   —EX. 23:12

When I was growing up in New York City, the so-called blue laws legislated what we could and could not do on Sunday. For example, liquor could not be purchased before one in the afternoon, we could not start noisy work before ten in the morning, and retail stores were closed. For most people today, though, Sunday is just like any other day with church thrown in.

It is probably an understatement to say that you cannot be successful in business today and work a forty-hour week. Most corporations demand sixty- or seventy-hour weeks from their executives.

Right now I'm on enforced leave from my job because I burned out. It's still hard for me to believe, but tough, hardworking, and always responsible, I have run out of steam. I've been on a reduced schedule for a month now and am thinking more clearly. I take a walk every day and spend quality time with the Lord. So take it from me, take time out once a week to rest up.

God, thank You for giving me my health today. Remind me to spend time in recreation, in appreciating Your creation, and with You in prayer and meditation.

T. S.

Wait on the LORD;
Be of good courage,
And He shall strengthen
your heart.
—PS. 27:14

We commonly believe that we should alleviate all physical and emotional pain. As kids we were taught that pain was unacceptable. Most of us were taken to a doctor at the first sign of illness or injury. We saw our parents lie down if they weren't feeling just right; take a pill if they ached; take a drink if they were upset.

One reason addictions are formed and maintained is to medicate pain. Many men attempt to anesthetize themselves through drugs. Some men accidentally get addicted to drugs as the result of work-related injuries and continue to take them in order to function or return to work. Others become addicted to drugs or alcohol by taking a drink of alcohol or a hit of marijuana after work to relax.

In the Middle Ages men did not have pills or drugs for every little pain. Enduring pain was a virtue and a sign of strength. Maybe we can find the "real men" inside us as we face our own pains of life.

Do not let your body rule your mind.

L. S.

My son, hear the instruction of your father,
And do not forsake the law of your mother.
—PROV. 1:8

Not all parents provide good instruction. But some do. God has given parents an innate desire to want the best for their children. Many try to teach basic principles that will help the child find success in his life, even though they may not provide all the help and guidance perfectly.

Parents provide a source of learning for children. God encourages us to listen and to heed our parents' teachings.

Steven came to counseling after spending time in prison. He shared that his parents had tried to raise him in a godly way. He learned right from wrong under their teaching. But he chose to forsake their instruction and was arrested for stealing construction equipment to sell for drug money. He wept as he confessed how he longed to have lived the life his parents instructed him to live.

What about your life? Do you live it as your father and mother instructed you to? Do you live it as your heavenly Father instructed you to?

God, help me to be the son who honors my parents' names and Yours.

B. N.

As for every man to whom God has given riches and wealth, and given him power to eat of it, to receive his heritage and rejoice in his labor—this is the gift of God.   —ECCL. 5:19

When I was drinking, I hung around the local tavern. One topic of conversation around the bar was work— that awful place we have to go to work for that so-and-so of a boss. We always seemed to know the right way to run the company if we only had the chance.

After I sobered up and stopped going to bars, I realized that conversation at home is often about work. Here, too, work gets a bum rap. The supervisor is unkind, unfeeling, or just plain stupid.

Even among Christians, I hear how difficult it is to go to work every day, how Christian organizations don't pay enough, and on and on.

But what does God say? He says His gift to you is to have riches and wealth and to enjoy them. He says that He will give us the ability to accept our lot in life and be happy in our work.

Just for today, list the things about your work for which you are grateful. Then thank the Lord for your work and for His gift of your job.

God, thank You that I have work to do today. Thank You for my work. Give me happiness in my work, as You have promised.

T. S.

Fathers, do not provoke your children to wrath, but bring them up in the training and admonition of the Lord.

—EPH. 6:4

Young children are vulnerable and impressionable. Children are also capable of sexual feeling at a very early age. In fact, a child's first sexual experiences formulate his sexual experience for life. If our children hear us talk about sexual matters openly at a young age, they are affected. If they see Mommy and Daddy kissing and hugging, this is good. But seeing Mommy and Daddy having foreplay in the living room can be harmful. The young child cannot process such a sexual encounter. Slang words for sex can negatively affect children, but being so scrupulous that you convey that sex is bad can be almost as unhealthy.

If you are a father, be aware of the sexual boundaries that exist between you and your children. Many children have been victims of covert sexual abuse because their fathers had no boundaries.

Lord, show me the boundaries that I need to set with my children.

L. S.

Let not your heart be troubled.
—JOHN 14:1

Every day you can find a new study or opinion on the heart and its "state." It seems that nothing is safe for our hearts. It also seems that too much exercise is as bad as too much food. Oh, the heartburn.

What's my cholesterol count? How much fat have I had today? Do I get enough fiber? Now I'm worried.

So many things could harm us. But there are guidelines to follow. Sensible diet and exercise are primary. We can also reduce stress. We may start by not being consumed by what could happen but instead living healthily based on what we know.

When God instructs us to not let our hearts be troubled, He is telling us basically to rest in His comfort and peace; not to bring on any undue stress. We do this by reminding ourselves of what we do know. First, if you are a believer, you *are* going to heaven. Second, you have a great weapon in prayer. Third, you know you are loved. Finally, you know the God of peace. As we remember these, we find comfort and a trouble-free heart.

Father, I acknowledge that You are the source of peace and serenity. Help my heart find rest in You.

B. D.

*Take what is yours and go your way. I wish to give
to this last man the same as to you. Is it not lawful
for me to do what I wish with my own things?*
—MATT. 20:14–15

A minister friend of mine tells this story: Some years
back he was called to a new church, which had suffered from discord and difficulties. Yet the church pros-
pered, attendance doubled, and many were blessed by
its ministry. One day a woman in the church who was
in the hospital called and asked to see the pastor.

When he visited her, she asked if someone could
take over her job in the church. Sheepishly my friend
asked her what her job was.

"Three years ago, when you first came to the
church, I knew we were troubled. I committed to stay
up all night on Saturday to pray. Now I'm no longer
able to, and I need someone else to take over."

My friend concludes, "That woman's prayer had
more to do with our church's success than any of the
work I did."

What is your yardstick for measuring the value of
work? According to the Scripture, God's viewpoint
may be less production oriented, less efficient than our
own.

*God, help me to see my work and the work of others through Your
eyes. Help me to use Your yardstick when evaluating others' work.*

T. S.

"Be angry, and do not sin"; do not let the sun go down on your wrath. —EPH. 4:26

How some men deal with their anger has always fascinated me. Rather than admit to anger some men give other explanations: "I'll be okay—I'm just a little frustrated"; "I was irritated"; "I was just concerned"; and "I was just hurt." Several men have gotten angry at my telling them I thought they were angry.

Anger can be difficult for several reasons. A man may have been taught not to get angry. If he was raised in a violent home, he may have decided to avoid all conflict. Showing anger may signal loss of control or a sign of weakness. A man may actually fear he will do or say something regrettable.

You can learn how to handle anger effectively. First, God gave man anger to get his needs met. Without anger a man could not have any control over his life. Getting or being angry is okay. The way we express anger is our concern. Anger occurs in degrees and can range from mild irritation to homicidal rage; so hurt, jealousy, impatience, disappointment, and grief may represent different degrees of anger. And anger does not go away with time. If we fail to acknowledge our anger and deal with it, we will ultimately act it out in an unhealthy way.

Remember, the question isn't whether a man expresses his anger, but how.

L. S.

Trust in the LORD with all your heart,
And lean not on your own understanding;
In all your ways acknowledge Him,
And He shall direct your paths.
—PROV. 3:5–6

Let's face it. We men struggle with the idea of following others. We want to be sufficient in ourselves. Sometimes we feel that to acknowledge weakness or need for others is not what a real man is supposed to do.

My daughter thinks I can fix anything. She tells her mother that she wants Daddy to fix it (whatever happens to be broken at the time) when he gets home. One day the lights went out while she was home with her mother. I happened to call at that time. While I was on the phone, the lights came back on. My daughter's response was, "Daddy fixed it!" Sometimes the man's role in family and at work seems to be that others are leaning on us.

It's great comfort to me to know that there is someone I can lean on. Even if there isn't another human person who can support me, God can. He wants me to lean on Him, and He wants to give me the direction I need. I can lean on God for direction and for fixing life's little problems in much the same way my daughter leans on me.

Lord, help me to trust You today with the paths of my life.

B. N.

*Do not labor for the food which perishes, but for
the food which endures to everlasting life, which
the Son of Man will give you. . . .*

—JOHN 6:27

I'm in "full-time Christian service." I work for a nonde-
moninational, nonprofit organization. Certainly I
should be able to discern between the food that perishes and the food that endures. But often I can't.

Like anyone else, I wax hot at the thought of reaching people for Jesus, at accomplishing great deeds on
Christ's behalf. But often I find myself concerned with
the food that perishes.

Are you like me? I hope so because I hate to be alone
in admitting poor performance.

Today I'm going to keep track of what kind of food I
work for during the day. When I go to bed tonight, I'll
ask the Lord to help me pursue the food that endures.
Anybody want to join me?

*Lord, thank You for Your provision of food that perishes, which we
need. Help me to watch for opportunities to work for the food that
endures.*

T. S.

> *The LORD is my rock and my fortress and*
> *my deliverer;*
> *My God, my strength, in whom I will trust.*
> —PS. 18:2

Frank was thirty-five and had worked for a major corporation for fifteen years. He had been in middle management and was quite comfortable financially at fifty to seventy thousand a year.

In my office, Frank did not appear to be doing so well. He had been laid off for approximately six months. He went from making seventy thousand to making nothing. His wife did not work outside the home. To make it worse, Frank had put off working on his savings plan. When he looked for work, he was either underqualified or overqualified. To save the little he had, Frank had to take a position at twenty-five thousand; he lost his home; and he lost many of his supposed friends.

Maybe you have had to go from the executive suite down to the factory. It is a severe adjustment, but it can be done. You first must grieve and accept the loss. Your priorities and values, your lifestyle and friends will change. Although it is devastating, it is also possible to adjust, start over, and rebuild.

Although you have lost a major cornerstone in your life, God will hold you up.

L. S.

We ought to obey God rather than men.
—ACTS 5:29

There are many great preachers and good books out there today: men with keen insight and incredible charisma; books giving practical advice. I went to a fellowship not long ago and I overheard a conversation: "Well, my favorite preacher is _____ and he really speaks to me. I've also been reading _____'s latest book, and I believe everything he's saying is right on. Who have you been reading?"

There was a long silence, and then as if embarrassed the responder said, "Well . . . God. I've been reading God, the Bible."

This reply just stopped me in my tracks. Its honesty spoke volumes. While it is good to read good books and listen to great preaching, we must never put them above our holy God and His holy Word.

We look for great men to lead us, men of godly character and humility. But what we must always remember is that these are still men, fallible and human. They may lead and teach us, but never should they be mistaken for God. Books, too, may be of great value, but they should never replace God's Word.

Listen to good preaching and read good books, but live in response to God and God alone.

Father, You are almighty God, the creator of the universe. There is no one greater.

B. D.

*And the fire will test each one's work, of what
sort it is. If anyone's work which he has built on it
endures, he will receive a reward. If anyone's work
is burned, he will suffer loss.*

—1 COR. 3:13–15

My friends tell me I'm in midlife crisis. I seem to be
paying more attention to what I'll leave behind. I'm
forty-five, never married, twenty pounds overweight,
hard of hearing, wear glasses, and have the best teeth
money can buy. I have an average intellect and an intense disposition. I love the Lord and hope to leave
something of value behind when I go to be with Him.

As I take inventory of my life so far, I'm not impressed. The first thirty-three years were spent mostly
drunk. I hurt myself and a lot of people around me. A
lot of the last twelve years has been spent in repairing
the damage.

I see opportunities to leave something behind more
often than I take them. But when I do seize the opportunities, I feel fulfilled. I'd like to be remembered like
Barnabas: "He was a good man, full of the Holy Spirit
and of faith. And a great many people were added to
the Lord (Acts 11:24)."

---

*God, help me to be more like Barnabas. Help me to seize my oppor-
tunities to serve You.*

T. S.

Do not boast about tomorrow,
For you do not know what a day
may bring forth.
—PROV. 27:1

The threat of falling back into the addiction cycle is real for anyone in recovery, no matter what the addiction might be or how long he has been in recovery. One of the lies of addiction is that the longer a man avoids or sustains, the more control he has. While this belief pattern is easy to slip into, it is an illusion and temporary at best. When a man begins to feel that sense of control, he has begun to fall back into the belief system that fed the addiction in the first place.

Interestingly enough, current research on addictions supports the idea that addictions continue to progress even in recovery. Many who relapse after two to five years of sobriety end up acting out worse than before recovery. It is as though the addiction says, "I'm going to give you a break and not bother you for a year or so; but the day is coming when we're going to make up for lost time."

The illusion of control keeps one blind to the power of his addiction and seduces him into relapse. A man must constantly stay humbly aware that the addiction is still alive and well.

Remember that pride comes before the fall.

L. S.

> *What profit has the worker from that in which he labors? I have seen the God-given task with which the sons of men are to be occupied.*
> —ECCL. 3:9–10

Not only do men struggle with the belief that what they earn (monetary from the world) equals their worth; sometimes they struggle with realizing that what they earn is a gift from God. Because we naturally believe that everything we make comes from ourselves, it requires an effort to remember that it comes from God. Too many men don't want to share what God has blessed them with.

I watched my godly father give money faithfully back to God each week. There were times when he couldn't really afford to give that money. God blessed his giving and continues to do so today.

Men need to be willing to honor God for the blessings they work for. One way to honor God and show Him that you realize that everything comes from Him is to give gifts back to God.

Father, help me to be a godly man by honoring You from my wealth.

B. N.

*And whatever you do, do it heartily, as to the Lord
and not to men, knowing that from the Lord you
will receive the reward of the inheritance; for you
serve the Lord Christ.* —COL. 3:23–24

I began working full-time when I was twenty years old. I worked for an airline in the freight business. Of course, we had a union, and I quickly got a position of shop steward. I thought I was terrific. The idea, you see, was to get paid as much as I could for doing the least I had to. I was pretty good at it, always making sure, though, that I talked a good job.

My attitude toward my supervisors and superiors was contentious and demeaning. I undercut their authority as often as I could. I abused my sick time and other benefits.

Satisfaction escaped me, however. I took nice vacations, bought nice cars, lived well, but satisfaction eluded me.

One day things changed. Through a series of experiences, I came to realize that I was really working for the Lord. I began to be more responsible with sick time, to work harder at getting to work on time, to be more respectful of my superiors, and genuinely to try to cooperate.

And I began to be satisfied. I was a responsible employee . . . responsible to the Lord.

*Lord, whatever my work today, help me to be responsible . . . to You!
Thank You for my work and the opportunity to serve You through it.*
T. S.

> *Seek first the kingdom of God and His*
> *righteousness, and all these things shall*
> *be added to you.*
> —MATT. 6:33

Most men have a deep fear of failure, often unseen because it is embedded within and protected. Since it is unacceptable for men to show insecurities, we put on the macho image and live as though we have no fears.

We fear that we're not going to be able to provide for our families or to leave our mark on society. We fear that we're not going to live up to the family legacy or our own expectations.

I tell myself that I have only failed when I have failed to try. And I can fail without being a failure. There are also different degrees of failures and failure experiences.

All men today will experience the feelings of falling short. When we fail God, ourselves, or others, we can condemn ourselves—tell ourselves we're no good—or we can accept our humanness, our imperfection, and God's grace. We can continue to love ourselves even though we have fallen short.

You have only failed when you have failed to try.

L. S.

*But God demonstrates His own love toward us, in
that while we were still sinners, Christ died for us.*
—ROM. 5:8

For Steve, there was no question who the most important player on the field was. It was his son. Steve could
tell you every detail of his son's performance. The
team's uniforms were all the same color, and it seemed
that everyone looked the same. Steve, however, could
pick his boy out of the crowd. He knew his walk, the
way he carried his head, even the way he twiddled his
fingers. This was his son. He's seen him grow from a
crawling infant to a budding man and knows his
quirks, knows his pain.

When a father sees his child, that's all he sees. There
is no one else as special, no one else as loved. God sees
all of us in the same way. It's incredible to know that
out of billions of people alive today, God sees us individually with that kind of love. God loves us all
uniquely and unconditionally, cheering for us throughout our lives. The greatest example of His love was giving up His only Son for all of us.

*Father, may I always be mindful of Your love for me, unconditional
and all-accepting.*

B. D.

*Admitted to God, to ourselves and to another
human being the exact nature of our wrongs.*
—THE TWELVE STEPS OF ALCOHOLICS ANONYMOUS

*There will be more joy in heaven over one sinner
who repents than over ninety-nine just persons
who need no repentance.*   —LUKE 15:7

I waited until the last to tell the worst. Slowly I began to talk specifically about my sexual misconduct. After I finished, Art said, "Well, that wasn't so bad, was it? Now go home and do the sixth and seventh steps."

When I began telling Art all this awful stuff about me, I really thought I might die. Instead, as I left his house, I began to feel a little freer than I had ever felt before. Someone knew all the terrible things I had done and did not reject me. What a feeling!

The work that began with Art that night continues twelve years later. I find more things that I need to tell to someone who will stand in God's place and honor my repentance.

When I share out of my own perverted heart, the angels rejoice as I free myself from guilt and pain.

God, thank You for the power of sharing our darkest thoughts with another man and with You. I pray You will encourage me to continue to be honest as I grow in You.

T. S.

If the ax is dull,
And one does not sharpen the edge,
Then he must use more strength;
But wisdom brings success.
　　　　　　　　—ECCL. 10:10

Imagine for a moment that you own a very large company. You have an opening for a general manager, a very high position. You have selected a man whom you have worked with for years and tell him that the job is his if he wants it. To your surprise he looks at you and says, "I'm flattered, but I must turn it down because I just don't think I can handle it."

You would probably be surprised if someone told you he was afraid to have it all. Who would be afraid to have all the money they needed, a plush job, prestige, and high social status? Surprisingly many men are afraid of reaching certain levels of success. Most of the time this fear is hidden because it is not acceptable for a man today.

Some men are afraid because they think that if things get too good something bad will happen. Others believe they do not deserve success and are not capable of achieving it, so they sabotage any success they have.

To enjoy the fruits of success, you must first deal with the part of you that wants you to fail.

_____

Remember that any success you have is actually not your own, but God's.

　　　　　　　　　　　　　　　　　　　L. S.

Do not withhold good from those to whom it is due,
When it is in the power of your hand to do so.
—PROV. 3:27

Men are not known for their expressions of affection or for giving compliments. In fact, we are often criticized for withholding compliments. You've heard the story of the man whose wife of thirty-eight years asked him if he loved her. He answered, "I told you I loved you thirty-eight years ago when I married you—if I had changed my mind, I would have told you."

Men are becoming aware of how important it is to speak words of affection and encouragement to our loved ones. Fred was beaming after hearing a word of praise from his boss. The words Fred's boss spoke took only a matter of seconds, but they increased Fred's interest and commitment to his work dramatically. We need to be aware how important it is to praise and encourage the others in our lives.

What words of encouragement and support can you share today? What can you say to your spouse? Your children? Your boss? Your employees? Your friends?

Lord, help me to pass along goodness today to those around me.

B. N.

*And whoever exalts himself will be abased, and he
who humbles himself will be exalted.*
—MATT. 23:12

I was at my usual Thursday night AA group. Dave, his smiling face exuding confidence, said, "I really can't explain it, but something happens when I dump all my garbage in front of another person; we become better friends!"

What Dave said came out of his own rich experience. I trusted him and knew he wouldn't lead me astray. So Dave gave me the confidence to do my first really honest fifth step.

Over the years I have done many fifth steps and listened to more than a few. In every case, we were better friends after we shared. Sharing our common struggles draws us together, makes us love another more, tells us we are more like one another than different.

I still see Dave at meetings. And I will never forget the confidence he gave me to try that first honest fifth. I hope he has encouraged you as well.

God, thank You for people who share out of their experience and for the love that comes out of the fifth step.

T. S.

> *I am the vine, you are the branches. He who abides*
> *in Me, and I in him, bears much fruit; for without*
> *Me you can do nothing.* —JOHN 15:5

Have you ever asked yourself, Who am I? Why do I exist? What is the meaning of life? These are existential questions of life.

Your answers to these questions depend upon how well you know yourself and how well you know God. One who doesn't know God will likely answer that the meaning of life is found in pleasure. To this man all meaning ceases after death. For the man who knows God, the meaning of life is found in God and focused on the eternal. This man's significance is forever connected to God's plan and purpose.

Today men are looking for significance and meaning in all of the wrong places: achievement, wealth, notoriety, power, control, and knowledge.

These beliefs could not be further from the truth. Many millionaires and CEOs become severely depressed and want to take their lives. Enduring significance can only be found in Christ. Jesus said that man cannot live by bread alone.

Lord, help me to remember that apart from You I am nothing.

L. S.

The inward man is being renewed day by day.
—2 COR. 4:16

How many of you have a favorite chair or couch? The kind that wraps itself around you and seems to smother you with comfort? On any given football Sunday, as soon as I get out of church, I'm headed for my pampering place. Initially it's just a nice place to sit, but the longer I stay on that couch, the more comfortable I get. There's no challenge to this, the couch expects nothing, and I'm not harming anyone—what could possibly be wrong? Through the course of the afternoon I have gone from a full slouch to an all-out recline. Just when I have reached slothful bliss, my wife may ask me to do something that would require my moving, and I inform her that I'm just too comfortable to move. You can only guess how helpful I seem to my wife on these occasions.

Our Christian walk can fit the same pattern. Initially we enjoy the new experiences of a faith in Christ, but all too quickly we can become comfortable, not wanting to do anything. In other words, not wanting to be bothered. Moving out of our comfort zone requires work and effort. Is your couch of complacency holding you back from getting involved, or are you alert and eager to answer God's call?

———

Father, I pray for renewal in my heart that I may battle the comfort of complacency.

B. D.

Do you have faith? Have it to yourself before God.
Happy is he who does not condemn himself in
what he approves.
—ROM. 14:22

Nothing made me more uncomfortable than to have someone say something nice about me, especially to my face. I just couldn't believe that anyone would recognize anything good in me. I knew I was bad.

After my hospitalization for alcoholism, I was put in a support group that met every Wednesday night. One night I was late for my group. As I entered the room, only one chair was vacant in the circle, and that was clear across the room. I had to walk in front of everyone seated in the circle. As I neared the center of the circle, the group leader said, "Ted, do you know what I see when you come into the room? I see a really fine person."

My heart sank and my faced flushed as I sped to the safety of the vacant chair. *How could she say such a terrible thing to me? How sarcastic!* I thought to myself.

The fifth step is like my little story. You will be surprised to learn that you are not as bad as you think.

God, please help me see the good in myself, not just the bad. Thank You for a chance to see myself as You see me.

T. S.

*Examine yourselves as to whether you are in the
faith. Prove yourselves. Do you not know
yourselves, that Jesus Christ is in you?*
— 2 COR. 13:5

One of the most often missed dynamics of recovery is
the dynamic of personality.

Why is personality an important dynamic in recovery? The Twelve Steps point out that an addict possesses certain personality or character defects, which
are to be monitored and removed on a daily basis.
These character defects refer to a man's inner struggles with control, impatience, intolerance, procrastination, jealousy, manipulation, isolation, perfectionism,
and many others. In recovery it is essential that a man
deals with the defects in his personality daily, because
it is a man's personality makeup that determines how
he responds to his world. For example, if a man is intolerant and perfectionistic he is likely to be angry and
frustrated all of the time, since no one will ever live up
to his standards. Being angry and frustrated too long
can certainly turn into an excuse to have occasional
drinks for tension relief.

It is through the daily inventory that provisions are
made for the continual adjustment of a man's personality. If a man prays for the mind of Christ daily and continually monitors himself in an honest way, making
necessary personality changes, he can experience a
very positive recovery process.

Lord, I pray that my personality will be a reflection of You.

L. S.

> *Flee sexual immorality. Every sin that a man does*
> *is outside the body, but he who commits sexual*
> *immorality sins against his own body.*
> —1 COR. 6:18

Hank never intended to be another marriage statistic. He didn't even realize that he wasn't all that happy in his marriage. He befriended a woman at work. Before he knew it, he was involved with her sexually. She was very understanding while he was going through tough times. She seemed to understand his work-related problems; he didn't realize he had stopped sharing them at home. Even when he knew that he was getting too involved with his friend at work, he did not flee the situation, and his failure led to immorality. His decision has destroyed many lives, not just his own.

Like Hank, many men are in marriages that they don't feel satisfied about. This makes them vulnerable to sexual temptation. The sexual sins are not just affairs, but include pornography, homosexuality, and other ways to cover up the emptiness inside. Sexual sins take a strong hold on a man's life. Fleeing is the best solution. If you're in it too far to flee, seek help. Don't let sexual immorality destroy your life.

Father, give me the strength to resist temptations to immorality.

B. N.

I will arise and go to my father, and will say to him, "Father, I have sinned against heaven and before you."
                                                    —LUKE 15:18

It took a lot of courage for the prodigal son to admit to his father that he was wrong. After all, he had his pride. But being reduced to eating food for pigs, suffering greatly far away from home, made it possible. And I am like him in many ways.

When I did the fifth step the first time and even when I do it now, it required that I give up some of my pride, that I admit I was wrong or had hurt someone or was not a very nice guy. I admit to my heavenly Father that I have made mistakes.

Another problem the prodigal faced was his father's reaction. He couldn't imagine complete pardon or forgiveness. For him it would have been good enough to be a servant. And I struggle with that too. How can God accept me as a son, without reservation, after some of the things I've done or thought? Yet He does, every time, without exception. And He'll do it for you, too!

God, thank You for Your complete acceptance of me when I am honest with You. Give me courage to be honest when I take the fifth step.

                                                                T. S.

> *Or do you not know that your body is the temple of*
> *the Holy Spirit who is in you, whom you have from*
> *God, and you are not your own?*
> —1 COR. 6:19

Many of us are fighting what I call "the battle of the bulge." I'm referring to the surge of fat that attacks many of us at the waist and under the chin.

With the exception of men who exercise compulsively, men have not taken physical fitness seriously. Most of us were fairly fit in high school and college. When we got married and got into the career fast track, we lost it.

We spend more time working, thinking, traveling, and sitting at computers and desks than we do in physically exercising. We are junk food and fast food junkies. Since we are home less and have less time, breakfast is often MacDonald's or a Hostess™ cupcake; lunch, a burger; and supper, maybe a late pizza. We also tend to be so tired from work that we want to relax, sleep, or watch TV in our spare time.

In restoring our physical fitness we must gain a balance in our lives, changing our eating habits, working less, and putting in a fair amount of exercise time. Our bodies are temples of the Holy Spirit.

Lord, help me to respect the only body that You have given me.

L. S.

How can a young man cleanse his way?
By taking heed according to Your word.
—PS. 119:9

The man was of good reputation and great intellect. He had left his mark in history by more than just "words." He was admired, for he knew the value of respectful consideration and work. We continue to live with the fruit of his labor even today. It is probably of little concern to people how this man lived his life. But it was of great and considerable import to him—so much so that he wanted others to know. Daniel Webster said, "If there is anything in my thought or style to commend, the credit is due to my parents for instilling in me early love for the Scriptures."

Many great men have shone in history, and for many the sentiment is the same. The Scripture was instrumental in shaping their lives. From Abraham Lincoln to Sir Isaac Newton, the Bible was a source of light in times of darkness and a guide for life.

What place does God's Word have in your life? In times of change and stress it is truly life-giving water, cleansing and revitalizing.

_____

Lord, I pray that Your holy Word would be my guide for living and source for encouragement.

B. D.

*For the weapons of our warfare are not carnal
but mighty in God for pulling down strongholds,
casting down arguments and every high thing that
exalts itself against the knowledge of God, bringing
every thought into captivity to the obedience
of Christ.*

—2 COR. 10:4–5

Weapons in our arsenal—that is what the Twelve Steps are. And they are indeed mighty! The fifth step cuts through years of silence about ourselves, of pretending that everything is okay. It gives us humility so that we can continue with the sixth and seventh steps to arrive at full repentance. And it gives us a sense of how much we have in common with the people around us.

While the fifth step is intimidating, it is also a breath of fresh air as we open the long-closed storage locker of everything that bothers us about ourselves. We can be assured that we have begun a good work, tearing down the stronghold of deceit that has reigned in our lives. Thank God for this formidable weapon of honesty as we begin the new life in Christ.

God, thank You for providing me with the fifth step. I pray that I will use it to break free of the past and join You in the pursuit of happy destiny.

T. S.

. . . bringing every thought into captivity to the obedience of Christ. —2 COR. 10:5

The more you tell a man he cannot have something, the more he will want it. This was true in the Garden of Eden where God told Adam and Eve that they were not to partake of the tree. Satan used this very warning to stir up their curiosity.

We men are easily beset by our own sexual curiousities. We tend to lust after experiences we perceive to be untouchable or unobtainable. The very inability to possess only produces more burning sexual desire within. Since Christian men are not supposed to give in to these desires, abstaining produces psychological distress, and giving in produces spiritual distress.

Remember that sin only lasts for a season. Afterwards, we usually feel guilt and shame. At times of sexual temptation, I tell myself that one hour or one day of pleasure isn't worth a lifetime of pain. Examining the cost of giving in to your lust can often reduce its power.

God, help me to foresee the consequences of giving in to my lust.

L. S.

> *"I have made a covenant with my eyes;*
> *Why then should I look upon a young woman?"*
> —JOB 31:1

Men are tempted every day. Our eyes are tempted with the visual stimulation that the world provides. TV ads, billboards, and magazine pictures all entice us to take our eyes off God.

We need to make a covenant as Job did. It's a covenant with our eyes. We need to covenant to look at those things which are good. Marty came to counseling because he was struggling with an addiction to pornography. He lusted with his eyes over magazine pictures, advertising pictures, and so on. He suffered enormous guilt and shame. Part of his recovery was to make a covenant with his eyes to flee tempting pictures and situations. This was an important step in overcoming his addiction to pornography.

You can't help being tempted in our world today. You can covenant where you will rest your eyes. You know what you need to avoid. Keep your eyes safe from sexual temptation.

Lord, I commit my gaze to be on You. Help me to keep my focus on You.

B. N.

*. . . but, speaking the truth in love, may grow up in
all things into Him who is the head—Christ.*
                                        —EPH. 4:15

Like Peter Pan, I never wanted to grow up. That's not as unusual as it sounds. Many men have the "Peter Pan syndrome."

I wanted to be grown-up as far as personal freedom was concerned, but wanted no part of personal responsibility. That, after all, is serious business. I might make mistakes or cause problems, but most of all I might not get everything I wanted if I had to grow up. And getting everything I wanted was very important to me!

Being grown-up, or at least acting that way is very important when working the steps. The fifth step in particular asks me to be responsible and to take myself and my problems, God, and another human being seriously. There is no room for childishness on the fifth step.

God, help me to approach the steps in a grown-up way. Help me to take myself, You, and someone else seriously when I do the fifth step.
                                                          T. S.

Put off, concerning your former conduct, the old man which grows corrupt according to the deceitful lusts, and be renewed in the spirit of your mind.
—EPH. 4:22–23

The secrecy of sexual abuse is tragic and painful. It is in many ways worse for the perpetrator. The perpetrator must live with the knowledge of what he did. He constantly wonders if anyone knows or is going to find out the secret. He must always live with the knowledge of how his abuse affected the innocent victim, be it his own or another child. If it is his daughter and she has not told, then he must always be afraid that his wife will find out. He must always live with the fear of how God feels about his secret, always obsessing over whether or not to tell.

If you have ever abused someone sexually and have kept it a secret, get healing. You will never experience a happy day until you tell. And the victim may never get help until you do tell. Confession can free you of your guilt. You may have to pay a penalty, but you will gain your freedom.

———————

Tell the truth and set yourself and the victim free.

L. S.

For what will it profit a man if he gains the whole world, and loses his own soul? —MARK 8:36

Profit margin," "the bottom line," "the secret of success"—all of these are thrown around in today's competitive business trenches. Everyone, so it seems, wants a few more dollars or a couple more properties. Lately, though, the evening news has shown us that behind all the hype and business sense of Wall Street, some men are crashing down the empty shaft of money and possessions. These men made a choice that was shrouded in glitz and glamor but in reality was hay and stubble.

What can money bring to a soul? Peace? No. Fame and power are only temporary, and prosperity lasts only until we see someone with more.

Satisfaction and fulfillment lie in following Jesus Christ. The hard part may be staying in line. If we see profit from an eternal perspective, we position ourselves to experience riches far greater than our wildest imagination.

Real profit is to experience and possess what money can't buy.

Father, help me to realize that my passion should be for things money can't buy.

B. D.

> *Therefore, putting away lying, each one speak*
> *truth with his neighbor, for we are members of*
> *one another.*
> —EPH. 4:25

When I have the privilege of hearing someone else's fifth step, I am always humbled by his choosing me to listen to his most recent attempt to tell all to God and another man. That humility forces me, as he continues with the process, to share some of my past and present struggles with him.

Until I read this Scripture, I didn't know what to call my feelings when I did this. I knew that there was a closeness, a bond, a sense of belonging to the human race. But the verse makes it clearer: "We are members of one another."

What a sense of relief! After years of isolation, of going it alone, we belong. We belong to God's heavenly family through Jesus Christ. And we can feel it, for the very first time, as we break down the walls that have separated us for so long from our fellow man. We have a place in the world. We fit in!

God, thank You for that powerful medicine called the truth. Allow me to continue the process so that I may truly know that I belong.

T. S.

*Whoever commits adultery with a woman
lacks understanding.*   —PROV. 6:32

The grass is greener on the other side"—so Frank believed when he had an affair after fifteen years of marriage. He found his secretary was more sexually appealing than his wife. He could talk more intimately with his secretary than he could with his wife. He felt revived and regenerated by his secretary. He was infatuated by his secretary's youth and charm, and she made him feel young again.

Frank divorced his first wife for his secretary and lost custody of his three daughters. The first six months were exciting, but this euphoria ended quickly as his fantasy bride left a note saying, "It was nice while it lasted, but I've found someone else that I love."

Frank is now forty-five, lives alone, is alienated from his wife and kids, and has been divorced twice. He told me how he longs to be back with his first wife and three daughters, but he can no longer be a part of their life. Was the affair worth it?

Lord, be my shepherd and keep me from greener pastures.

L. S.

> *Be doers of the word, and not hearers only,*
> *deceiving yourselves.*
> —JAMES 1:22

I know a few men who love to inflict their knowledge on any willing victim. Have you ever been caught by one of them? They seem to know everything and can talk as an expert on any subject. Many times I get the feeling as I listen to them that they are deceiving themselves because their lack of real expertise comes out in the things they share.

One way to become a true expert on a subject is to have experience in it. Recovery is not possible without applying the things you are learning. Roger was in counseling for codependency. He came faithfully week after week and listened to the information I shared with him. He knew a great deal about codependency, but he wasn't making any progress in counseling. He wasn't getting better, because he wasn't applying the knowledge to his life.

You need to practice what you are learning and apply it day by day.

Lord, help me to be a doer of Your Word today.

B. N.

*Confess your trespasses to one another, and pray
for one another, that you may be healed.*
—JAMES 5:16

I have a confession to make: My family was prejudiced, universally prejudiced, with a bias against anyone who was different. Roman Catholics, for some
reason, were especially singled out for the "bias bar-
rage."

Essentially, everything that we thought Catholics
practiced was worthy of our attack. It was particularly
easy to criticize confession. To our enlightened protes-
tant minds, the concept of telling all to a priest and
receiving forgiveness from him was particularly ab-
horrent. God and God alone provided forgiveness—
everyone knew that!

What we failed to appreciate was the healing power
of confession as set forth in this Scripture, the spiritual
cleansing that came from unburdening ourselves of
deeds or thoughts that separated us from God.

The essence of the fifth step is confessing, sharing
with another human being so that we both may approach God for healing forgiveness.

*Father, thank You for the healing that comes from Your unfailing
forgiveness. I pray I might approach the fifth step with enthusiasm
for the healing that will come through it.*

T. S.

> *The LORD is my rock and my fortress and*
> *my deliverer;*
> *My God, my strength, in whom I will trust.*
> —PS. 18:2

Work is one of our longest and most taxing lots in life. And some have it even harder. Some men have to work with handicaps—blindness, chronic pain, confinement to a wheelchair, or even illiteracy.

Society has not done a very good job of ministering to men with handicaps; therefore, working, for the handicapped male, is made even more difficult. If you are struggling with a handicap or disability you know by now how hard it is to face work. You must realize that being handicapped does not change your worth in God's eyes. Your perceived weakness or loss may be the very strength or gain that someone else needs to experience. By isolating yourself you help no one. Your own deficit allows you to give in ways that others cannot.

If you are handicapped and you have given up the fight, realize that you can still be a man and you can still contribute. Reentering the work force will give you a renewed faith in your manhood and a more peaceful spirit.

———————

Lord, give me the courage to go on when work seems unbearable.

L. S.

*He who has My commandments and keeps them, it
is he who loves Me.* —JOHN 14:21

As children we were instructed to obey our parents.
Mostly, we did knowing all too well the consequences
of disobeying. We also obeyed them because we loved
them and knew that they loved us. We sought approval, and by obeying, we got it. Kids who display
consistent disobedience have never effectively connected with their parents.

What is our proof of love for the Savior? Just as in a
child, it must be obedience. Obedience shows the
world that we take our faith and our God seriously. God
the Father requires and deserves our respect, love, and
appreciation. A child's obedience should be a natural
response to a loving father.

Do people see your love for the Father through your
obedience to Him?

Consider 2 John 6: "This is love, that we walk according to His commandments."

Father, let my obedience be a testimony of my love for You.

B. D.

> *If we confess our sins, He is faithful and just to*
> *forgive us our sins and to cleanse us from all*
> *unrighteousness.*
> — 1 JOHN 1:9

Confession is appealing only if we look at the result and not the act itself. It might be compared to going to the dentist. Going to the dentist is uncomfortable, inconvenient, and possibly even threatening, but we want healthy teeth and know the dangers of neglect.

How do we become convinced that the fifth step is as good for us as going to the dentist? My friend Bob tells this story: "I was around the program for about a year and couldn't seem to get the courage to do the fourth and fifth steps. Then one night as we were having coffee, three other men at the table took a napkin and wrote this on it: 'We, the undersigned, guarantee to Bob F. a positive result for doing the fourth and fifth steps. If it is not so, we will cheerfully refund his misery free of charge.' I have done the fourth and fifth steps many times since then, but I still have that napkin to remind me of those three men's loving concern for me."

God, thank You for the loving testimony of other men. I pray You will encourage me to work on myself through their example.

T. S.

*Come to Me, all you who labor and are heavy
laden, and I will give you rest.* —MATT. 11:28

Unfortunately, most male sex abuse victims never recover because they are usually too ashamed to tell
anyone. They just go on letting the shame poison their
lives and maybe ultimately committing suicide. But
men who do ask for help and get into recovery find
great hope for healing the wounds.

In the first stage of healing you acknowledge that
sexual abuse has occurred. Maybe a teenage boy made
you do sexual things with him or a babysitter fondled
you. Maybe an older man made you perform sex acts
with him when you were young. You must tell yourself
what happened and then tell someone else, usually a
therapist.

You next enter the stage of anger and rage, which
must be expressed in a therapeutic way to the abuser
or abusers.

The next stage involves grief work over the loss of
certain relationships, innocence, identity, and years of
adulthood happiness.

Finally you learn to channel your negative energy
into self-improvement. Ultimately, you are able to forgive and move from being a victim to being a survivor
with the benefits of recovery.

---

*As you work through the stages of grief you open the doors
to healing.*

L. S.

> *For Ezra had prepared his heart to seek the Law of the LORD, and to do it, and to teach statutes and ordinances in Israel.*
> —EZRA 7:10

Ezra set a good example for men in recovery. He set his heart to study God's Word. He then practiced it, and finally he taught it.

As a man is working through the recovery process, it is important that he studies the principles involved in recovery. He then must practice them and finally must teach them to others.

I have a friend who has been involved with recovery for over twenty years. He began by studying and practicing the material. Now he is teaching it to others. How important that we study, practice, and teach—in that order.

Father, help me be a student to the truths You have for me.

B. N.

You cannot serve God and mammon.
—MATT. 6:24

Everyone in this country must have heard this verse at some time. In my church we all adhered to the idea of putting the Lord before money, but I'm not sure we really did it!

It's hard, after all. The mail carrier regularly brings glad tidings from the electric company, phone company, doctor, and of course, the Internal Revenue Service. In fact, my friend Bill is sitting behind me right now, sorting through a big stack of bills. How can I not be concerned with money?

Yet the sunrise this morning cost me nothing. Little Mary, Bill's four-year-old daughter, smiled at me last night. Only cost me a vanilla cone at the Dairy Queen! No amount of money could provide the good health I have today . . . God did that!

The key seems to be remembering that God is my provider. Maybe I should put a little note inside my checkbook that says, "Don't forget who gave you all this."

Lord, thank You for Your provision for all my needs. I pray that You will make me more responsible in my use of the money and property You have provided.

T. S.

Lying lips are an abomination to the LORD,
But those who deal truthfully are His delight.
—PROV. 12:22

Harry was a compulsive exaggerator and liar. When Harry closed a thousand-dollar deal, he called it a ten-thousand-dollar deal. When asked about his college education, he claimed years of college when he had only a few semesters.

Harry also told white lies. When his employer asked him if he had called on a client, Harry would say yes even though he hadn't. When his wife asked if he was going to be late from work, he would say no even if he knew he would be.

Men usually tell white lies or exaggerate to avoid conflict, rejection, or reproof; to get attention; or to appear greater than they actually are. Harry grew up with a rejection-sensitive spirit. He learned to avoid retribution by lying and to get positive strokes by exaggerating. These character traits followed him into adulthood.

Harry recovered after about two years of therapy. He had to face his shame and abuse issues; learn to accept himself; and learn how to tell the truth. If you relate to Harry's story, the only way out for you is honesty.

———————————

The truth may hurt, but it will set you free.

L. S.

> *The effective, fervent prayer of a righteous man*
> *avails much.* —JAMES 5:16

We depend on communication—effective communication. In relationships we can see its value in how close two people are. Rarely, if ever, will you see a good relationship when two people do not communicate. Communication is the highway we take to understanding another person while also hopefully being understood. In true communication both people must take part; both must be present.

Sadly, our culture seems to put a low price tag on effective communication. We have become a society of expediency. Whatever happened to face-to-face interaction? There is nothing more appealing to a customer or stockholder than the opportunity to speak directly with the CEO.

Prayer is communion with God. This is the case of the stockholder speaking directly with the CEO or, in this case, the owner. God has given us this avenue to share our needs, wants, hurts, and appreciation. This is not some company suggestion box. Prayer is the joining of two, God and His child. Prayer is essential for the relationship, for without it the Christian never excels. Prayer is more than words; it is an expression of love toward God.

Father, thank You for the privilege of prayer and the promise that You hear me.

B. D.

And He said to them, "Take nothing for the journey, neither staffs nor bag nor bread nor money; and do not have two tunics apiece."
    —LUKE 9:3

Jesus told the disciples to travel light. That's what this verse says to me. And if I am to imitate the disciples, I should probably be traveling lighter than I do.

You see, I travel often on business. Two bags always go with me. Lots of money, in the form of a few credit cards, and sometimes even a snack goes along as well. Good news . . . I never take a staff!

Seriously, what was Jesus telling the disciples about money in this command? I think He was reminding them—and me—to keep our priorities right. I think He was telling me to remember why I was traveling, whom I serve day and night, who gives me sustenance, including my next breath, and who provided the staff, the bread, the money, and the tunics.

Christ wants me to use well what He has given me. In short, Christ asks me to depend on Him. He will provide for me . . . if I ask Him!

Lord, thank You for reminding me today to rely upon You. I pray I will remember You when I travel out each day to work Your will.

    T. S.

*But godliness with contentment is great gain. For
we brought nothing into this world, and it is certain
we can carry nothing out.* —1 TIM. 6:6–7

Every man who has ever identified himself as an addict has experienced the "black hole," a feeling of emptiness shared by men who struggle with addiction. This emptiness is often experienced as a deep depression, fear, isolation, and loneliness accompanied by a burning desire to fill the mysterious void. It ultimately manifests itself as a constant need for stimulation.

A man who lives with a black hole will seek to gratify himself through every means possible: He works long hours, starts new projects, or engrosses himself in television, exercises, or reading. When the emptiness still haunts him, he may drink, take drugs, gamble, masturbate, or overeat.

Actually, only a few experiences are authentic enough to fill the deep sense of emptiness. These are an unconditional love for self, true intimacy with others, a healthy relationship with God, and a consistent and legitimate meeting of one's physical, social, emotional, and spiritual needs.

Lord, help me to strive after the things that are unseen.

L. S.

> *His delight is in the law of the Lord,*
> *And in His law he meditates day*
> *and night.*   —PS. 1:2

The recovery process involves stopping to meditate on the truths that God has for you. Meditating involves digesting the truths and making them an active part of your life.

John gives a great deal of credit for his success in the recovery process to the fact that he meditates on God's Word every day. God's Word reinforces the positive changes he is trying to make in his life. It inspires him and stays with him throughout the day. God's truth has gotten into his mind and his spirit, and it energizes him to be the kind of man God wants him to be, even when his circumstances haven't changed.

Meditating on God's Word doesn't have to take long periods of time. It does take making His Word a priority in your life. The results are sure to give you direction and energy from God Himself.

God, help me to stop today and meditate on Your greatness.

B. N.

And Joses, who was also named Barnabas . . . a
Levite of the country of Cyprus, having land, sold
it, and brought the money and laid it at the
apostles' feet.   —ACTS 4:36–37

Some years ago, my sister and I invested in some "surefire, can't-miss" stock recommended by a friend. We bought at eighteen and watched it rise steadily to thirty-five. "Let's sell it," I said.

"No," she said, "it will go higher."

Recently we sold the stock for three dollars a share. Let's talk about giving money away, but not the way my sister and I did it.

The first time Barnabas appeared in Scripture, his generosity was highlighted. He sold what he owned and gave the money—all of it—to the disciples. He surely would be blessed for such generosity, so what was his blessing?

Well, he spent time in jail, suffered with Paul, and put his life on the line for Christ more than once. Hardly sounds like a blessing.

I think the description of Barnabas in Acts 11 was his blessing. I covet that description for myself. It gives the rewards of a generous man: he was good, full of faith, full of the Spirit of God, and fruitful.

God, thank You for providing for me today. Help me to be generous as Barnabas was.

T. S.

> *The LORD is my strength and my shield;*
> *My heart trusted in Him, and I am helped.*
> —PS. 28:7

When we think about or hear about sexual abuse, we tend to think about little girls who were sexually abused by some grisly, perverted old man at the park. An even worse form of sexual abuse is called incest, sexual relations between blood relatives. It may occur among extended family members and is not exclusively limited to intercourse.

More than 90 percent of male victims never come forward. Male victims usually feel that they were responsible or should have done something.

Male incest victims may have been manipulated into sexual encounters with family members. The abuse may range from the stroking of his genitals to full intercourse. Abuse also occurs when an abuser does anything to or with the boy to gain sexual arousal.

Maybe you do not realize that you are an incest victim. You may have thought that early sexual experiences with family were normal. You may have also been told to never tell anyone. If you feel uncomfortable about a sexual memory and you've never resolved it, you may be an incest victim.

Let go of responsibility for the abusive events of your childhood.

L. S.

Jesus wept.
—JOHN 11:35

There was never a question about how strong Dale was. Standing 6′4″ and weighing close to 300 pounds, he was a big man. His reputation in sports and his physical attributes were known for miles around. Everyone said he was "a man's man."

Late one summer Dale's father died. When he got the news, he was surrounded by several people, all wondering how he would respond. Some even stepped back, fearing that this big man, this "man's man" would break out in a rage. Much to their surprise, though, Dale slowly fell to his knees and wept without the least bit of shame or embarrassment. He was weeping appropriately, lovingly. This may have been his greatest strength, the strength and self-assurance to show his emotions.

The shortest verse in the Bible is John 11:35, "Jesus wept." But this verse may have the greatest impact for men today. No longer are we shackled by the lies of "manhood" but instead free by the gift of emotion, the honesty of tears.

If Christ our Savior and Lord wept, we humans then have all the more reason to do the same.

Lord, help me to know that my emotions can be my greatest strength.

B. D.

Now all who believed were together, and had all things in common, and sold their possessions and goods, and divided them among all, as anyone had need.
—ACTS 2:44–45

How would you handle this? One Sunday your pastor, Reverend Smith, gets up and declares, "We're going to pool our resources. All of us will declare all we have, in money and property. We will give all our money to the church treasurer. We will sign over title to all our property to the church. If it was good enough for the first century church, it's good enough for us!"

You probably would hope your new pastor wouldn't have such radical ideas. Yet the first-century Christians did just what Reverend Smith suggested. Can we learn from that?

I suggest that we look at our attitude. Can we stand honestly before God, with everything we have in our outstretched arms, and say, "Here, Lord, is everything I own. Take it all if You need it." That attitude will mesh perfectly with the attitude of those early Christians. And we all will be the richer for it.

God, thank You for providing everything I have. Please take it today, if You need it. All I have is Yours if You want it.

T. S.

As a loving deer and a graceful doe,
Let her breasts satisfy you at all times;
And always be enraptured with her love.
—PROV. 5:19

One line I hear in response to a question about infidelity is, "No, we didn't commit adultery—we didn't have intercourse." This line is shared with pride and a sense of accomplishment. The men who say this are usually surprised to hear that they have committed adultery.

Sexuality is transgenital. It transcends the mere act of sexual intercourse. Our sexuality involves every aspect of our being and can be expressed mentally, physically, and emotionally. Have you ever shared intimate secrets with a woman other than your wife or had more emotional intimacy with a woman other than your wife? Have you had other forms of physical contact with a woman other than your wife such as kissing, hugging, fondling, masturbating, or exchanging sexual innuendoes? If so, you may have committed emotional as well as physical adultery. And these covert sexual behaviors lead to deeper and more overt sexual acts.

When things are not going well in marriage, it's easy to rationalize covert sexual behavior with other women.

Try to be faithful to your wife in all ways.

Lord, help me to be faithful to my wife in all ways.

> *Therefore we also, since we are surrounded by so great a cloud of witnesses, let us lay aside every weight, and the sin which so easily ensnares us, and let us run with endurance the race that is set before us.*
>
> **—HEB. 12:1**

Recovery is like a race. We are trying to get through life without becoming sidetracked. It's important to have people cheering for you as you run the race.

Several people in my life have been there to cheer me on when things were rough. Each has cheered in different ways and for different reasons, but their cheers kept me on the path. I think of my high school buddies who cheered me with words. I also think of the people who believed in me through college. A special woman who believed in me sent me money to pay my seminary tuition. Today, my needs for cheering are different, and God provides cheerers in different ways. There are my wife, my young daughter, my boss, my friends.

Each of us has a race to win. Each of us needs to have a support group of people who cheer us on when we are discouraged.

God, give me people to cheer me on as I run the race to victory.

B. N.

He who loves silver will not be satisfied with silver;
Nor he who loves abundance, with increase.
This also is vanity. —ECCL. 5:10

When I was drinking, my attitude about money was simple: How do I get enough to buy the next drink?

After I got sober, my attitude began to change. I saw money as the way out of my problems. I was in debt, so I needed money to clear it up. I lost weight and needed money for new clothes. I realized my car was an old clunker, and I needed money for a new car.

The more I thought I needed money, the more I needed money. Should I get a second job (not a good idea for an alcoholic in early recovery)? Maybe I should complete my education and get a better job. Of course, completing my education would take money, lots of money. Whatever I did, there was never enough money.

One day I realized how much money would be enough. All the money in the world . . . plus one dollar. If money was my first priority, I would never have enough money.

All my money comes from God. As I prayed to change my preoccupation with money, I realized one thing: When my bills are paid, when I have something to give to the Lord's work, when all my needs (not my wants) are taken care of, that's enough. The Lord provides for me as I seek to know His will for me.

God, thank You for giving me what I have. Help me to remember that enough is enough.

T. S.

> *He is despised and rejected by men,*
> *A man of sorrows and acquainted with grief.*
> *And we hid, as it were, our faces from Him;*
> *He was despised, and we did not esteem Him.*
> —ISA. 53:3

It's easy to feel insignificant at work. If you're just one employee out of thousands, most of whom are over you in authority, you can feel that you are never considered in any decision made at your job. After all, no one ever comes to ask you your opinion. Going through the I.D. checkpoint and having to pass security can make you feel like a nobody or just an I.D. number.

Feeling insignificant is like being a small fish in a big pond. You never get to eat much because the big fish get all the food. You are afraid all the time because you are unsure if you are going to be eaten by a bigger fish. But your importance really depends on how you look at it. Putting a part on an F-16 fighter plane right seems more significant to me than a Pentagon meeting of the top aircraft builders.

We are all part of a bigger body, though—the body of Christ. He alluded to the fact that every part was important, no matter how small it was.

The most important contributions in life often go unnoticed.

L. S.

Casting all your care upon Him, for He cares for you.
—1 PETER 5:7

On February 8, 1990, a new life was brought into this world. Like all new fathers I was overwhelmed. This fragile little being, so dependent, so needy. But I was somehow convinced that I was ready for this responsibility. My love made me "feel" ready, that I would do anything in my power for this precious soul. Through the months, however, I have come to a painful realization of my own limitations. There will be times and situations that I won't have an answer or a solution. I may be inadequate.

It would be easy for us to think that we can be all things to our family, that we have the power to handle every situation—physical, mental, and emotional. The truth is we can't. But we have a heavenly Father who can. When we stop and consider His awesome power, wisdom, and love, we find comfort. Understanding that we don't have to be superhuman gives us the freedom to live within our humanness and rely on an ever-present, always loving God.

Father, help me to see You as the source for all of my needs.

B. D.

> *Let your conduct be without covetousness, and*
> *be content with such things as you have. For He*
> *Himself has said, "I will never leave you nor*
> *forsake you." So we may boldly say:*
> > *"The LORD is my helper;*
> > *I will not fear.*
> > *What can man do to me?"*
> > —HEB. 13:5–6

In my first few years of sobriety, I worried about money. How could I earn more? Where could I get more? It was on my mind all the time.

One day I was talking to my sponsor, telling him I thought I would die if I didn't have a certain thing, something so important that I can't remember now what it was. His simple reply: "Well, die then!"

That comment went right to the heart of it. I wouldn't really die if I didn't get everything I wanted. Why, I wouldn't even get sick. I started to realize that I had everything I needed and a lot more.

During all these years, I have never really wanted for anything. I haven't slept a night on a park bench, haven't missed a meal, haven't been without work for very long, haven't been without friends . . . I have always had everything I needed.

God, thank You for providing for my needs in great abundance. I pray that my attitude will continue to be more centered on You and less on material things.

T. S.

Nevertheless, because of sexual immorality, let each man have his own wife, and let each woman have her own husband.
　　　　　　　　　　　　　　—1 COR. 7:2

What is the apostle Paul saying about sex? Is he saying that sex is bad and that single men are to resign themselves to lives of celibacy as eunuchs? No.

Paul was writing a letter to the church of Corinth to answer questions about asceticism. The ascetics basically believed that those who abstained from physical contact were somehow more pure or holy than those who did not. Paul quickly corrected them, telling them that sex and marriage were okay. He stated that not all men had the gift of celibacy such as he did and that it would be better for them to marry than to burn with lust and commit fornication.

If you find that you have a strong sexual desire for women, you should be thinking about marriage in your future. It would actually be better for you to be in a committed marital relationship than for you to continue to lust and struggle with sexuality.

For the Christian male premarital intercourse and petting only serve to create guilt and a lack of respect between both partners. Most couples I talk to tell me that they wish they had waited.

Lord, help me to abstain sexually until I marry.

　　　　　　　　　　　　　　　　　　　　L. S.

> *Reject profane and old wives' fables, and exercise*
> *yourself rather to godliness. For bodily exercise*
> *profits a little, but godliness is profitable for all*
> *things, having promise of the life now is and of*
> *that which is to come.*   —1 TIM. 4:7–8

Part of the recovery process involves discipline. We must be disciplined not to take that drink, buy that magazine, call that number. The Bible encourages us to discipline ourselves for the purpose of godliness.

I see this lived out by my good friend. He works hard to be disciplined in the things of God. He meditates on Scripture, prays, and enjoys fellowship with other believers. He often states that the discipline for the purpose of godliness has paid off in his family life and business life. It appears that way to me.

When we discipline ourselves spiritually, it often enters other areas of our lives as well. It doesn't come naturally to do the things of God. It requires practice and determination. But the payoffs are more than worth the investment in godly discipline.

God, strengthen me with the discipline to be a godly man.

B. N.

For men will be lovers of themselves, lovers of money, boasters, proud, blasphemers, disobedient to parents, unthankful, unholy, unloving, unforgiving, slanderers, without self-control, brutal, despisers of good, traitors, headstrong, haughty, lovers of pleasure rather than lovers of God, having a form of godliness but denying its power. And from such people turn away! —2 TIM. 3:2–5

And from such people turn away!" Good idea! Paul paints a grim picture of how men will be in the last days. And it's not surprising that love of money makes the list—it has to do with idolatry.

God hates idolatry. He wants nothing to come between us and Him. He makes that very clear in the Bible. And by definition, love of money qualifies. I have written six other times about money in this book, and the common thread is this: Love of money makes it impossible to depend on God for our needs.

And if we are lovers of money, can all the other despicable character defects that Paul mentions be far behind? If I start to compromise myself in finances, will I also not become proud, unthankful, unholy, unloving, unforgiving? I need to be very careful that my self-centeredness doesn't drag me into love of money.

God, thank You for providing for all my needs. Help me to keep money in its right place.

T. S.

Two are better than one,
Because they have a good reward for their labor.
For if they fall, one will lift up his companion.
But woe to him who is alone when he falls.
—ECCL. 4:9–10

The act of intimacy with another person involves self-disclosure. In fact, it has often been said that the level of intimacy with another is directly proportional to the level of self-disclosure with its high risk of openness and vulnerability. Addicts are often so alienated from their own feelings that they almost can't connect with others at a deep level.

The addict's struggle with intimacy in relationships grows out of strong core beliefs:

1. I am a bad and unworthy person.

2. Anyone who knew who I really am wouldn't like me.

3. I cannot depend on anyone to meet my needs.

4. So I must depend on my addiction.

The addict's belief system is reinforced by a thick outer wall of guilt and shame. No wonder loneliness and isolation are common symptoms of all addictions.

Breaking the cycle of isolationism involves adopting a new belief system as well as breaking down the guilt and shame wall.

Lord, help me to share openly with significant others.

L. S.

> *But Daniel purposed in his heart that he would*
> *not defile himself with the portion of the king's*
> *delicacies.*
> —DAN. 1:8

Several years ago I heard a fantastic sermon by Charles Stanley. It brought to light a very important question: "Am I a person of preference or conviction?"

Preference means that if I find myself in a situation that could be inconvenient or difficult, I would choose or look for a way out, basically saying, "I prefer to do something else, so I will." This may be safe but it isn't always right.

Conviction, on the other hand, says, "If I'm in a situation, no matter what the consequences, I must follow God's direction."

Daniel found himself in a unique position. Just a young man when he was taken captive, he was mature beyond his years. As you read the first chapter of Daniel, you'll see that he had a choice and could have gone the "preferred" route, but he "purposed" in his heart and stood by his convictions, bowing to no one but God.

Taking a stand based on conviction may not always be easy, but its rewards are worth the effort. It is the right choice to make.

Are you a man of preference or a man of conviction? God seeks men of action based on conviction.

B. D.

> *Were entirely ready to have God remove all these*
> *defects of character.*
> —THE TWELVE STEPS OF ALCOHOLICS ANONYMOUS

> *Shall we continue in sin that grace may abound?*
> *Certainly not!*
> —ROM. 6:1–2

I was always looking for the magic cure, the quick fix, a gimmick. Perhaps you have done the same. Sorry, but I have found no loopholes in God's plan.

If I approach the sixth step with the idea that I can get off the hook for past misdeeds, that I can be somehow galvanized into some nearly perfect person who will "go and sin no more," I will be sadly disappointed. There is no substitute for honesty and forthrightness. We must be entirely ready to have God remove these defects of character.

"But," I hear you say, "I've never been entirely ready for anything in my whole life." Neither have I. But we can ask God to help us be willing! Wherever we hold back, are afraid, or just aren't thinking clearly, we can depend on God to help us. We can have God's help even in becoming willing to change!

God, I don't always understand what's wrong with me and what needs changing. Help me today by making me willing where I need to be, and give me Your assurance of that help.

T. S.

The soul of a sluggard desires, and has nothing;
But the soul of the diligent shall be made rich.
—PROV. 13:4

Mary sat in my office telling me of a strange oppression that had overcome her husband of ten years. He had been quite vivacious: "I couldn't keep up with him." She also shared with me that her husband had always been willing to take her places and help her around the house.

Then Mary said, "My husband isn't the man I married. He won't go anywhere with me unless I beg him. He gets angry if I ask him to do anything around the house. He lives for the couch and the television. If we try to talk with him, he just tunes us out. The kids don't understand what's wrong with their father."

Mary's husband had become a victim of laziness. He never intended to have an affair with the couch; he was gradually seduced.

Lying in a recliner and watching television can be a pleasant change from the daily rat race. But the inactivity that accompanies this syndrome ultimately robs a man of motivation and creates a pattern of constant tiredness. If you are struggling with this syndrome, be very conscientious about the amount of time you spend with your family.

Lord, help me to be a good steward of my time.

L. S.

> *The angel of the LORD encamps all around*
> *those who fear Him,*
> *And delivers them.*
> —PS. 34:7

Many times in recovery we feel alone and scared. No other person can work through our pain. Sometimes the pain cannot even be shared with a friend because it is so deep in our soul. As a boy I remember going off to camp for the first time. As night fell I became scared. My friend who was sharing a tent with me was trying to comfort me. He encouraged me to look outside the tent and see all the other tents around us. When I did, it helped me feel more at peace. I figured that even if something bad happened, I would not have to face it alone.

At times we may feel alone while we are working through the pain that is often a part of the recovery process. God is camped around you today and wants to help you. You are not left alone to face whatever lurks in the darkness. His tent is close beside you, and He will never leave you.

God, thank You for being a caring friend who surrounds me.

B. N.

Blessed are the poor in spirit,
For theirs is the kingdom of heaven.
—MATT. 5:3

The first time I chaired a Twelve-Step meeting, I asked my friend Mary to speak on the sixth step. With a smile, she said, "So you want me to speak on the easy steps, six and seven." That was the first time anyone told me that these steps in particular are very hard. And so they are.

I do the sixth step formally every time I do a fifth step. The Big Book tells me that I should spend an hour or so reviewing all the things I have found objectionable, all the character defects I have uncovered. I must be sure I am ready to have God remove them.

"But why wouldn't you want these defects removed?" I hear you exclaim. There are several reasons, but pride comes to mind first: I somehow feel that it is up to me to legislate my behavior and emotions.

Here again, my friend Mary comes to the rescue. "We are problem people," she says, "and problem people make things difficult for themselves."

God, thank You for Mary's simple counsel and assurance. I pray that I may get pride out of the way when I do the sixth step.

T. S.

> *A man's heart plans his way,*
> *But the LORD directs his steps.*
> —PROV. 16:9

Many of us bring someone home from work with us each day. Those around us seem to be very aware of the stranger we bring home nightly. This invisible stranger eats dinner with us, takes a shower with us, talks to the kids and wife. The family continues to tell the stranger to go back to his own home, but they say he never leaves.

Who is this stranger that we men bring home with us? This stranger is called "the job." When we come home, we walk through the door physically, but we're mentally still at work. We're either thinking of the next sale, the next meeting, or the problems of the day. Our children can notice that we aren't really all there. We look at them off and on as they talk to us, but if they asked us what they said, we probably wouldn't know. The wife realizes that something else is on our mind when we don't feel like talking or being intimate.

As Christian men we need to leave work at work. It is important to be totally home for our family, in body and in spirit. They need to know that they are more important than work. Besides, it is not physically or mentally healthy to eat, drink, and sleep work twenty-four hours a day.

Lord, guide me in the way You would like me to go with my family.

L. S.

For I am not ashamed of the gospel of Christ, for it is the power of God to salvation for everyone who believes.
—ROM. 1:16

Jim was twenty when he died. A car swerved into his path, and he died instantly. Just hours before, he was playing pool in the student center of a Christian university. Jim was not a student, but his father was a pastor and a part-time professor at the school. Jim was labeled as wild, a rebel, but no one really knew him. While it was true that Jim had a flair for the dramatic, it was all too clear that something was missing in his life and that he was crying out in his own way. Still, no one suspected or even considered the chance of Jim being unsaved.

It has been several years since Jim died, but few people have ever inquired about Jim's faith. I suspect fear of guilt keeps people from trying. There were so many opportunities to find out for sure, and even risk the embarrassment, yet no one took the chance. One has to wonder what Jim might say to that.

Sharing one's faith may be uncomfortable, but think of the consequence to those who never are exposed to it. Sharing your faith can make the difference between life or death—life in eternity with Christ or death, separate and condemned.

Today, don't assume anything, especially if it affects someone's eternity.

B. D.

> *I will liken him to a wise man who built his house*
> *on the rock: and the rain descended, the floods*
> *came, and the winds blew and beat on that house;*
> *and it did not fall, for it was founded on the rock.*
> —MATT. 7:24–25

The Big Book of AA likens the sixth step to building an "arch through which we will walk a free man at last." It is very important that we do the best job we can with the first five steps, and Step 6 gives us the chance to review the work we have done.

Have I really gotten to the heart of all my resentments, understanding that holding on to any may sabotage my progress? Have I really done all I can to uproot my fears? And have I been honest about all past misconduct of which I am guilty? If my answer is no, now is the time for me to redo my fourth and fifth steps.

If, however, I can answer yes, then I can proceed to the seventh step, asking God to remove this troublesome baggage from the past.

God, thank You for the opportunity to check the thoroughness of my work on the steps. I pray that my best effort will lead to a lifetime of communion with You.

T. S.

The LORD has established His throne in heaven,
And His kingdom rules over all.

—PS. 103:19

Every man instinctively needs to control. In fact, we are supposed to use our built-in control mechanism to meet our God-given needs. Without the ability to control, we would not be able to get food, water, sleep, or exercise. We would probably alienate others and would always be alone. And we would have no boundaries with others and no limits on our self-destructive desires.

However, some men lose control or overcontrol. Loss of control usually occurs when a man has an external locus of control. The way he feels, responds, and relates to his world is determined by what goes on outside himself. Mark's feelings were almost always determined by what his wife was feeling. If Mark's wife was angry, he was angry; if she was depressed, he had to make her happy. Mark needed an internal locus of control to help him remain relatively okay despite negative external events. He could achieve this control by working on his faulty belief system and by learning to surrender to the sovereignty of God.

Lord, give me the serenity to accept the things I cannot change.

L. S.

> *Two are better than one,*
> *Because they have a good reward for their labor.*
> *For if they fall, one will lift up his companion.*
> *But woe to him who is alone when he falls,*
> *For he has no one to help him up.*
>
> —ECCL. 4:9–10

Often in the recovery process men struggle with the idea that they can or should go it alone. Whether at the first step of recovery or after some time in the process, many men feel they have to make it on their own.

Solomon's words of wisdom about two being better than one have proven true over and over in the lives of the men I have worked with. Jim is one who thought he should go it alone. He decided to drop out of a support group. Soon he found himself struggling with many of the same old problems. He stated later that he did not realize what a strength the support group had been to him. He realized he had been foolish to think he shouldn't need a support group. When he returned, he encouraged the group members not to underestimate the power of support and encouragement the group provided.

Are you going it alone? Why? Do you think you shouldn't need a support group? We all need encouragement and support.

God, bind me together with friends who can encourage and support me.

B. N.

And do not be conformed to this world, but be transformed by the renewing of your mind, that you may prove what is that good and acceptable and perfect will of God. —ROM. 12:2

The thought of being transformed by the renewing of my mind is exciting, comforting, and frightening. When I first did this step, I wrestled with fear. Sure, I wanted life to be better and wanted the pain to stop, so the idea of God's comfort for me was very appealing. But what if my mind was transformed so much that I could no longer make my own decisions? What if I became a spiritual robot, with no will of my own?

Here again, my AA friends came to my rescue. "Don't worry!" they said half jokingly. "God will have His hands full just getting the right ideas through your thick skull. You're in no danger of being turned into a mindless slave." And they were right.

Even so, I acknowledge my fear of the seventh step in the sixth step so that I can ask God to remove the objectionable things from my life as fully and completely as is possible today.

God, thank You for friends who come to the rescue. Thank You for understanding my fear and helping me to overcome it.

T. S.

*Know that the LORD your God, He is God, the
faithful God who keeps covenant and mercy for
a thousand generations with those who love Him
and keep His commandments.* —DEUT. 7:9

I have known a handful of wise men. As I have carefully examined their lives in order to learn from them, I
have discovered that they have four characteristics.
Wise men walk close to God; they have a good sense of
humor; they give others the benefit of the doubt; and
they are loyal. One of these characteristics which has
enticed me the most is loyalty.

In today's society we do not see too many wise and
loyal men. In earlier times a man could count on another man's loyalty through thick and thin or until
death. Nowadays, we men have to question our loyalty
for one another. We have doubts about how far our supposed friends or employers would go for us during bad
times. Others may wonder if we would go a long mile
for them.

What has happened to the loyal man today? Where
is he? He is hiding; he is afraid to come out. Today we
men live in constant fear and insecurity, so we are first
and foremost loyal to ourselves. We will be loyal to a
friend until such time our neck is on the block; then we
sacrifice loyalty to protect ourselves. Will you be one
of the new breed of loyal men, or will you turn away
when the cost gets too high?

Lord, give me the strength to be loyal.

L. S.

Greater love has no one than this, than to lay down one's life for his friends. —JOHN 15:13

Memorial Day brings bittersweet memories to thousands of men across America, reminders of battle fields in faraway places and holidays spent far from family. The most stirring reminders, though, are of comrades fallen in battle. We occasionally hear a story of uncommon valor, of a man giving his life to save another.

Could any of us give his life for another? The vast majority of us will never experience that choice. We would all like to say, "Yes, I could do it," but none of us knows for sure. What would it take? Bravery? Incentive? Maybe. But for sure, love—uncommon love, supernatural love. This love, in an instant, puts others first.

With Christ as our example, we are brought somehow closer to an understanding of unconditional and sacrificial love, love that is based not on reciprocation or return but on Christlikeness.

Even though we are not expected to make this sacrifice, we are given a glimpse of heavenly love through the eyes of mere men.

Father, as I go through life, convict me of the power of love for my brothers and sisters as well as the degree to which it is to be shown.

B. D.

*For godly sorrow produces repentance to salvation,
not to be regretted; but the sorrow of the world
produces death.*
                              —2 COR. 7:10

In the hours after my first honest fifth step, while I wrestled with the sixth step, I experienced a feeling new to me: I had a sorrow for all of my misdeeds, all of my shortcomings, all of the misspent years that had gone before. It was not the first time I had felt bad, sorrowful, regretful, or guilty, yet it was different.

Perhaps we can say it this way. All my life, I had wallowed in grief, despair, and self-pity. That, I think, was the sorrow of the world. After I had been as honest as I could be with God, myself, and someone else, the pain was the result of the godly sorrow that produces true repentance to salvation. Since I had never felt it before, I had no way of knowing what it was.

Finally, when I do the sixth step, I need to remember that godly sorrow is not to be regretted, but treasured. It is the true sorrow that leads to repentance and salvation.

_____

God, thank You for providing me with godly sorrow. Help me not to regret it, but to learn from it and use it for true repentance.

                                        T. S.

For where your treasure is, there your heart will be also.   —MATT. 6:21

The two most predominant influences on the American family today are materialism and the "psychology of more." God has greatly blessed our nation. The frightening aspect of this is that America is very much like the Roman Empire. I am afraid that we could fall as the Roman Empire did. In addition, our country is going further away from God, as the family unit disintegrates under the pressure of these two influences. The New Age media bombards our families with the ideas that we can have it all, deny ourselves nothing, and always seek pleasure.

As we men have been caught up into the whirlwind of achieving wealth and obtaining possessions, we have sold the integrity of our families down the river. Our wives have become accustomed to having the best, and our children already want to be like Daddy. In falling victim to materialism and the psychology of more, we have turned from God, family, and nature.

As Christian men we need to get off the merry-go-round and get back to the life Christ would have us live. As Christians we are not to be conformed to the philosophies of this world. Learn how to enjoy time with your family and how to enjoy nature. Learn that the psychology of enough—contentment is possible.

Obtaining true contentment is impossible through the world and without God.

L. S.

Husbands, dwell with them with understanding.
—1 PETER 3:7

Husbands are told to know and understand their wives. In fact, you could look at it as being a student of your wife. What does she like, dislike, need, want? Do you know your wife's favorite color? Could you pick out a dress she would like? What are her dreams for the future?

Much of the marriage counseling I do focuses on helping partners understand each other. Many times we expect our partner to think like we do. But, when it comes to men and women, nothing can be further from the truth. You don't have to agree with or completely understand your spouse; just be aware of what she likes. For example, my wife likes me to bring her flowers occasionally. Now I find that is downright stupid. Who would want to spend money on something that is going to be dead in a few days? There may be many things I don't understand about my wife, but I know them and practice them anyway. It helps keep the love and excitement alive in our marriage. After all, I shudder to think what it would be like to be married to a person who was exactly like me.

Lord, I want to be a student of my wife. Help me understand her better today.

B. N.

*For the flesh lusts against the Spirit, and the Spirit
against the flesh; and these are contrary to one
another, so that you do not do the things that
you wish.*
        —GAL. 5:17

Let's face it! The sixth step is uncomfortable and elusive. Getting the willingness to change is as difficult as capturing lightning in a bottle. And I am the chief obstacle to doing my best job with it.

I don't mean to get in the way, but my flesh and spirit are in conflict with one another. My fear of change, fear of failure, pride, obstinacy, and self-centeredness get in the way.

If I have been driven through the steps to Step 6, then I have admitted powerlessness and unmanageability. I have given up any hope of achieving a sane existence except for the intervention of God and have made a decision to turn things over to Him. Finally, I have written and shared all the objectionable things about me with God and someone else. Coming this far means that my life as it has existed until now is no bargain. So in quiet desperation, we may simply say,

———————————

Here, God, take all of me and do with me what You will.

           T. S.

For the love of money is a root of all kinds of evil.
—1 TIM. 6:10

Today men are obsessed with money. We devote hours each day to counting our money; spending it; and figuring out how to make more of it.

If you ever get rich, you may find out that money is not a solution. The more money you make, the more time and effort it takes to manage it. If you have so much money that you can do anything you want or go anywhere you want, you may find that nothing excites you anymore. The more money you make, the more you have to lose if things go sour.

As Christians we need to realize that our money is God's money. We are to give a portion back to Him, a portion to the government, a portion to the family. I also believe that we are to leave an inheritance to our kids; give to the poor; help the sick; and save money for future needs.

_____

Remember that we did not bring anything into this world and we will not leave with anything.

L. S.

*And my God shall supply all your need according
to His riches in glory by Christ Jesus.*
—PHIL. 4:19

As Henry worked through his recovery, he began voicing fear of not having any source of significance. Through his life Henry would tell you that his addictive behavior was a result of a poor self-image and a personal sense of insignificance. The more insignificant he felt, the more he reached for "things." However, what he needed was not tangible. Henry needed a sense of worth.

The impetus that drives Henry strikes thousands of other people each year. And what is it? Need—the need for love, for fellowship, for acceptance. Many of you know the pain of chasing your worth in people and things and finding out all too frequently the fickleness and fleeting nature of both. We have to anchor ourselves on a rich provision and an abundant supply.

In recovery we will battle with feelings of insignificance, but we must know that God the Father has both provision and abundance. If we are looking for significance in love, fellowship, and acceptance, then run—don't walk—to God and "fill 'er up."

---

*Looking to God for our needs lessens our expectations of others and
allows us to experience true abundance, which He supplies.*

B. D.

> *. . . that you put off, concerning your former*
> *conduct, the old man which grows corrupt*
> *according to the deceitful lusts, and be*
> *renewed in the spirit of your mind.*
> —EPH. 4:22–23

A big dog was never let out of the yard. All his life, as people walked past the fence, he barked, protecting his owners' property. Children teased him from the other side of the fence, and he barked and jumped at them.

One day his owner left the gate open. When the children came and teased him, he ran swiftly to the open gate—then he stopped! He had never been out there and didn't know what to expect. So he stayed safely inside the fence, even though the gate was open.

I was like that dog when it came to the sixth step. I had always been in the yard of my own pride, selfishness, and fear. The thought of jumping the fence to something new was scary. But a combination of my desperate present life and the sane and satisfied lives around me in AA gave me the courage to try the new way.

Lord, help me to leave the yard for the big world outside.

T. S.

By pride comes only contention,
But with the well-advised is wisdom.
—PROV. 13:10

Have you ever said that you and the boss were good friends when you were actually not? Or, has anyone come to you and said that he knew a celebrity, but you knew that it was not likely? This behavior is called name-dropping. Everywhere you go there are name-droppers. They use everyone and anyone's name, as long as it is convenient to their cause. Name-droppers are easily recognized because all they do is drop names; they know so and so; or they walk with so and so; or they had dinner with you know who.

Name-droppers thrive on the names of others because they are very insecure. They feel extremely inferior inside. It builds them up if they can believe that they are truly friends of a rich or famous person, even if actually they are usually not. They drop names to make you feel less important or for you to see them as more important.

If you know that you drop names from time to time and exaggerate personal connections, then work on your self-esteem and try to have some identity apart from the identity of others. Your worth is equal to all others; there is no need to add to it.

Our security should rest in God and not in others.

L. S.

> *Fathers, do not provoke your children to wrath, but bring them up in the training and admonition of the Lord.*
> —EPH. 6:4

I recently talked with a successful businessman about his fathering. He began to weep as he shared the mistakes he had made with his children. His addiction to alcohol had affected his children very negatively. His son had run away from home to escape his abuse. Being willing to recognize the pain he had caused his son was the beginning of his recovery process.

Many times in working through the recovery process you may have had to face your failures as a father with your own children. A lot of the men I work with come to see they are inflicting pain on their children as it was inflicted on them by their fathers. This happens over and over, even to men who swore they would never repeat these negative patterns.

Stop and evaluate yourself as a father. Don't underestimate your influence in your children's lives. There may be things about yourself that you don't enjoy looking at, but honesty will promote better relationships between your children and you.

God, help me to be the father that my children need today.

B. N.

*Lay aside all filthiness and overflow of wickedness,
and receive with meekness the implanted word,
which is able to save your souls.*

—JAMES 1:21

Mike did a thorough fifth step with me. He spoke of his resentment for family members, friends, employers, and people in authority. He had an exhaustive list of fears that had been with him since he was a little boy. And he was guilty—sexual misconduct, robbery, willful destruction of property.

When he had finished, I strongly suggested that he follow the instructions in the Big Book of AA. He should go home and get quiet before God, reviewing all he had covered in the fifth step. And he should take time to say the seventh-step prayer, asking God to take all the offending stuff of his old life away.

Today, Mike isn't doing very well. I hear he's drinking and doing drugs just as he did before he came to Twelve-Step meetings. Why? Because instead of going home and doing the sixth step, Mike watched TV.

God, help me not to waste all the effort so far by neglecting the sixth step. Help me to forgo the short-term pleasure for the long-term gain.

T. S.

*Husbands, love your wives, just as Christ also loved
the church and gave Himself for it.*

—EPH. 5:25

The wife of a sexually abused male is in her own way
a victim. Although she was not directly abused she carries her husband's pain. In the majority of cases the
wife of the male victim isn't even aware that she is
marrying someone who has been sexually abused.
Most wives of male sexual abuse victims never find out
because the abuse is kept such a secret. Unfortunately,
those wives who do find out usually do so when the
husbands sexually abuse their children—or the wives
themselves.

If you are a male victim of child sexual abuse, you
must realize that your mate has likely been a victim of
the pain you brought into the marriage. She has had to
deal with your depression and irritability. She has
coped with your lack of ability to be intimate and your
social avoidance. She has always wondered why you
were never really happy and why you rarely wanted to
have fun with her. She has lived with your jealousy of
kids or your fear of getting close to them.

Your partner deserves to know the truth so that she
can realize that things have not been her fault. Write a
letter to her explaining how you were abused and how
it has negatively affected your dealings with her. Tell
her that you're going to get help and make life better
for her.

As you minister to yourself, don't forget your partner.

L. S.

If any of you lacks wisdom, let him ask of God,
who gives to all liberally and without reproach,
and it will be given to him. —JAMES 1:5

Buying a house is an extremely important event. I have so many things to consider and to do. I am also learning how much I don't know. And I really don't like asking questions for fear of being seen as ignorant. This is just as bad as answering a question incorrectly. Call it pride or ego—either way it doesn't help.

I've always heard that the only way to get an answer is to ask a question, no matter how ridiculous it may seem. There are a multitude of things that we don't know, but we don't ask to preserve our self-esteem. Of course, we will never gain any more knowledge or grow if we don't ask. In buying our house, we were blessed with a knowledgeable agent. He was there to answer our questions, to keep us informed. All we had to do was ask.

How true this is with our experience with God. There will always be things that we know nothing about. God is our source for that knowledge, but we have to ask.

———————

Lord, your thoughts are higher than mine but You offer wisdom to those who seek it.

B. D.

> *Humbly asked Him to remove our shortcomings.*
> —THE TWELVE STEPS OF ALCOHOLICS ANONYMOUS
> *LORD, You have heard the desire of the humble;*
> *You will prepare their heart;*
> *You will cause Your ear to hear.* —PS. 10:17

Humility is difficult for me, mostly because I'm afraid I don't know anything about it. I'm not humble.

If I have been thorough with the first six steps of the program, the result should be humility. If I have admitted that I really don't know how to handle life, if I have entered the process of turning my will and life over to God, and if I have admitted all my wrongs to another and to God, then I must of necessity be humble. In Step 7 I formally ask God to remove defects of character that stand in the way of my usefulness to Him and my fellowman.

I'm not one to speak of humility. But if I ever have any, it's when, contrite, repentant, and aware of my limitations and depravity, I approach God, asking Him to do for me what I cannot do for myself.

God, thank You for preparing my heart for the changes to come. I pray that I will be sufficiently humble for You to complete Your work in me.

T. S.

*For all have sinned and fall short of the glory
of God.*   —ROM. 3:23

The worst part about perfectionistic people is their
tendency to be critical when others are not perfect.
Yes, it is true that everyone probably has some degree
of perfectionism. But it need not destroy our lives,
cause us to be severely depressed, or make everyone
else miserable.

Perfectionists have to be their best at all times. So
they procrastinate or work compulsively to perfect
the task. Perfectionists have an internal critical par-
ent, who rules them with an iron rod of "shoulds"
and "oughts." They always believe that they could do
better.

If you are a perfectionist, you must accept the fact
that you can never be perfect. Only Christ was perfect.
You must realize the difference between perfectionism
and excellence. The man who pursues excellence can
accept failure and learn from his mistakes. He can enjoy periods of accomplishment and success. Give up
your goal of perfection today, and accept your humanness.

------

*Sometimes our expectations for ourselves are higher than God's are
for us.*

L. S.

> *For the eyes of the LORD run to and fro throughout the whole earth, to show Himself strong on behalf of those whose heart is loyal to Him. In this you have done foolishly; therefore from now on you shall have wars.*
> —2 CHRON. 16:9

A man told me about a situation he had been in recently. He had been struggling with sexual acting out with other men. Late one night he found himself sitting in a park looking for an opportunity to act out sexually. While sitting there he began to cry and think about how much he wished his father had cared about him. His father had died several years earlier without ever telling him that he loved him. As he was crying, he began to pray. Suddenly he felt God's presence, and the loneliness lifted. He left the park and avoided the temptation to act out sexually.

God wants to give us support. So many times we do not recognize the support we have in Him. In our times of desperation He is the best support we can ever have. He is available twenty-four hours a day to help you in your recovery.

God, help me to realize how strongly You want to support me in my recovery.

B. N.

Lord, You have heard the desire of the humble;
You will prepare their heart;
You will cause Your ear to hear.

—PS. 10:17

Mrs. Kehoe, one of those dear saints that come into our lives, took care of me when I was a child. She lived down the block and came regularly to help with the housework and with me. She had bad arthritis, was nearly blind from glaucoma and cataracts, and was hard of hearing. Simply getting out of bed was an act of courage for Mrs. Kehoe.

Being around Mrs. Kehoe, I grew accustomed to repeating myself. "Speak up, Teddy!" she would say. "I can't hear you." So I raised my voice. "Speak louder, son," she would say. When I yelled at the top of my voice, Mrs. Kehoe, finally hearing me, would say indignantly, "You don't have to shout, Teddy! I can hear you."

The Scripture for today says that God, unlike dear old Mrs. Kehoe, turns His ear to hear us, straining to hear every sound we utter. When we come humbly to Step 7, God turns toward us and says, "Speak, My son. I can hear you very well."

Lord, thank You for turning toward me to hear my every word. I pray You will encourage me to speak frankly in the seventh step.

T. S.

> *He who covers his sins will not prosper,*
> *But whoever confesses and forsakes them*
> *will have mercy.* —PROV. 28:13

People who feel guilty try to run from it—just like Adam and Eve when they first met God after the Fall. What is the first thing you do just after you do something wrong? If you are like most people, you look to see if anyone else is around, then try to regain your composure or look inconspicuous. These maneuvers accomplish nothing in terms of resolving the guilt. Instead, they create additional problems.

Running from guilt separates a man from God. A man may believe he has escaped, but he has really only dug a deeper hole. It is impossible to hide from God.

Running from guilt also creates deeper internal distress and further alienation from God. As unresolved guilt is buried in the subconscious, it turns to anger and finally depression.

We need to deal with our guilt. Spiritually we are to recognize it, then confess it to God, accept God's forgiveness and grace, and turn from our sin. Psychologically, we can use guilt feelings to learn where we stand with our conscience and value system.

Lord, help me to grow from the awareness of my own guilt.

L. S.

And when He had sent the multitudes away, He went up on a mountain by Himself to pray. And when evening had come, He was alone there.
—MATT. 14:23

A lot has been said lately about "drivenness." It seems that our culture places a high premium on over-doing it. We have become a people who just can't slow down. Granted there are times that we have no choice about working a few extra hours, and we do love our play time. But we have become trapped by excesses. Between too much work and finding time to play, we may be neglecting the very thing that sustains us—*rest*.

It's easy to "keep on keeping on." But at what price? Scripture speaks often of responsibility to home, work, and God, but it also speaks of balance. In balance we find rest.

Who in history did more in a shorter time with greater consequence than Jesus Christ? No one! And Christ placed time alone and rest as a high priority. After several hours of preaching and ministry to the five thousand, Jesus took Himself away from multitudes for a time of restoration and communication with the heavenly Father.

Lord, help me to know my limitations so I may be fresh and strong for Your service.

B. D.

> *Pray for one another, that you may be healed.*
> *The effective, fervent prayer of a righteous man*
> *avails much.*
> —JAMES 5:16

The seventh-step prayer begins this way: "My Creator, I am now willing that You should have all of me, good and bad." Why would we want to give God the bad part of us?

When I first met Marshall, he was mute. He never said a single word for the first month that he came to Twelve-Step meetings. He was scared into silence. Finally, after weeks of listening, he began to open up.

You see, Marshall thought he was a bad guy, different from all the rest of us. As he came and simply listened, he heard from imperfect people like me just how imperfect we were. We showed the bad part of us openly to Marshall. And the more Marshall saw, the more he saw that he was not different.

The bad in us that we give to God, our imperfection faced openly and honestly, is miracle material. We are all sinners in need of a Savior, imperfect people who work together to help one another.

God, thank You for using the bad in me to Your glory. Make me honest enough today to encourage someone to turn to You for help.

T. S.

Let no corrupt communication proceed out of your
mouth, but what is good for necessary edification,
that it may impart grace to the hearers.
—EPH. 4:29

Every man has an innate need to wield power. The man who feels powerless is dangerous, for he will do whatever he has to do to survive. Society functions with the exchange of power.

As a man you have innate power as well as power that other people and institutions choose to entrust to you. Some men use their energy or power positively. Others take their power to the negative extreme. A man can use physical power to unload a truck or to beat someone up. Or a man may use his mental power to manipulate others or to gain their respect.

The Bible is clear that we are not to use power for any evil cause but to promote mutual love, growth, and respect.

Lord, help me to have a loving power rather than one of intimidation.

L. S.

Cursed is the ground for your sake;
In toil you shall eat of it
All the days of your life.
Both thorns and thistles it shall bring forth for you,
And you shall eat the herb of the field.
In the sweat of your face you shall eat bread
Till you return to the ground,
For out of it you were taken;
For dust you are,
And to dust you shall return.   —GEN. 3:17–19

Men and women are different—physically and emotionally. And they were cursed differently by God.

Man was cursed in the area of adequacy. God told Adam that he would have trouble with his livelihood. Men struggle with many feelings of inadequacy. They cover up much of the struggle by self-protective means.

Recently I failed to accomplish a task that I had promised another man to complete. Because of my feelings of inadequacy, I avoided discussing the issue with him. I tried not to see him and did not return his phone calls promptly because I didn't want to be seen as inadequate. Finally, I confessed my failure to accomplish the task. He gave me some very helpful hints, and I was determined to do my best. After I finally finished the job, I thought about the days I wasted being afraid I would be found out.

God, help me face my inadequacies, and give me strength to not hide.

B. N.

Therefore do not let sin reign in your mortal body,
that you should obey it in its lusts.

—ROM. 6:12

I was lying face down, half on the bed and half on the floor. My face was in a puddle of blood. On my right arm was a gash three inches long. A similar cut ran across my lower back. I was slowly regaining consciousness. As my memory returned, I remembered falling in the bathroom. I still don't remember making it to the bedroom.

Gruesome, isn't it? And it happened to me. It wasn't the first time that something so grisly had happened. And it wouldn't be the last. As I read this Scripture, I realized that sin was reigning in my body then. These awful incidents were the working out of deliberate disobedience to God's Word.

But they were something else as well. First, I need these memories to remind me of my awful life before I came to Twelve Step meetings. It's important that I not forget, lest I return to the drinking, drugging lifestyle. Second, these memories show me how God has consistently looked after me, even in the years when I was disobeying Him. I am still alive because of the consistent intervention of God.

God, thank You for Your tender mercies to me when I was so far away from You. Keep my memories fresh, lest I forget.

T. S.

> Let us cleanse ourselves from all filthiness of the
> flesh and spirit, perfecting holiness in the fear
> of God.
> —2 COR. 7:1

Just as a man doesn't become an addict overnight, he doesn't relapse overnight. Relapse is a process, a series of unconscious mini-decisions leading up to a final major decision to relinquish control of the addiction. A gradual decrease in self-discipline accompanies a change in one's feelings, thoughts, attitudes, and behavior.

The emotional pain threshold is the degree of emotional pain and shame that preceded one's walk into recovery. When a man who is maintaining his sobriety allows himself to return to this pain threshold, he suddenly remembers the anesthetic benefit he received from his drug of choice. Once a man crosses this line, he forfeits his choice in the matter and will relapse.

Relapse can be avoided by gaining the self-discipline to maintain a personal inventory daily and by dealing with any issues that surface. In the daily inventory look out for relationship stress, prolonged negative emotional states, physical pain, loneliness, or boredom. Dealing with these issues daily keeps the emotional pain to a minimum.

Do not take your problems from today into tomorrow.

L. S.

A man who has friends must himself be friendly,
But there is a friend who sticks closer than
a brother.   —PROV. 18:24

A child may grow up with a multitude of friends. It seems, though, that the number of friends a man has diminishes dramatically as he gets older. It seems that men don't place a priority on developing friendships. This could stem from an erroneous perception that men are self-sufficient, in need of nothing or no one. We have as great a need and desire for friends as anyone. While close friendships do require vulnerability, we don't have to fear or run from them. Any time we get to know someone, we risk rejection and hurt. More often than not, though, we learn more about ourselves, gain confidence, and feel loved when we take that risk. We all need and want friends. Some we will keep for a lifetime; others we will lose along the way. Being friendly will draw others to us, enhancing the circle. Being friendly costs nothing, but the benefits can be life changing.

A final thought: It's no secret that friends will come and go and even let you down. But there is One who will never leave you and is closer than you could ever imagine.

Lord, let me be a friend to those in need and see You as my closest friend when I am in need.

B. D.

If any of you lacks wisdom, let him ask of God,
who gives to all liberally and without reproach,
and it will be given to him. But let him ask in faith,
with no doubting, for he who doubts is like a wave
of the sea driven and tossed by the wind.
—JAMES 1:5–6

How many things are you totally sure of, without any doubt? Think about it. After all, we live in a changing, inconsistent world where second-guessing is the norm. So how many things do you believe in without any question?

For myself, the list of things I have no doubt about is small: I believe there is a God, I believe Christ died for my sins, and I believe that I will go home with Him someday. I also have no doubt that I will at some time doubt everything else.

The seventh-step prayer, however, leaves little room for doubt:

My Creator, I am now willing that You should have all of me, good and bad. I pray that You now remove from me every single defect of character which stands in the way of my usefulness to You and to my fellows. Grant me strength, as I go out from here, to do Your bidding. Amen.

I can ask God to give me the willingness. God can do even that!

God, thank You for letting me borrow willingness from You. I pray that I may doubt less and less as I learn more about You.

T. S.

*"You shall love the LORD your God with all your
heart, with all your soul, and with all your mind."
This is the first and great commandment.*
—MATT. 22:37–38

If you were to inventory how you spend your time every minute of the day, what would you learn? How much time would be given to your family, how much to TV and videos, eating, exercise, work, or working on spiritual growth? Some men would be embarrassed by the results of their time inventory. They might realize that most of their time was spent on things that don't matter much.

Ideally a man's use of time should reflect his priorities. However, most of us usually have two sets of priorities: our ideal set and our real set. We like to tell people about our ideal set, but people most often see those values that are truly most important to us. Many of us claim that our family and God are the two most important and valuable factors in our lives, but this may not be reflected in the way we spend our time and set our priorities.

As Christians, our priorities should be God, family, work, self, others, and other things. And our use of time should reflect these priorities.

You have found the right priorities when they have become pleasing to God.

L. S.

> *Sanctify the Lord God in your hearts, and always*
> *be ready to give a defense to everyone who asks*
> *you a reason for the hope that is in you, with*
> *meekness and fear.* —1 PETER 3:15

As Christian men we have many opportunities to witness to people. The recovery process adds challenges and opportunities to share with others. Often people can see something different in us. The Scripture encourages us to be ready to explain what that difference is.

Recently, Rob told me he had been at a support meeting when afterwards a man came up to him and asked if they could talk. The man stated that he had noticed something different about Rob and wanted to find out what it was. Rob explained that he was a Christian and was able to lead the man to salvation in Jesus Christ. Rob had found his hope in a living Savior, and because of his availability, a man in need came to know that same hope.

The recovery process can provide an opportunity to share the gospel. Don't be afraid to share your hope.

I want to be available today to share the hope that is within me.

B. N.

Ask, and it will be given to you; seek, and you will find; knock, and it will be opened to you. For everyone who asks receives, and he who seeks finds, and to him who knocks it will be opened.
—MATT. 7:7–8

Al can't ask for anything directly. You know what I mean: He'll ask, "Are you going anywhere near Main and Wesley?" instead of, "Will you give me a ride home?"

Fear is at the heart of Al's problem—fear of rejection that comes from being hurt, from having been told in a thousand ways that he was worthless. And that fear causes him problems with the seventh step, as well.

Suppose Al does get the courage to ask God for help in the seventh step . . . and God refuses! The ultimate rejection! God has said that he's not worth saving. What a knock!

Now, we all know in our heads that God would never reject someone who sincerely asked Him for help. But do we know it in our hearts? It truly is a leap of faith.

Are you like Al? If so, then pray along with me. . . .

God, I am fearful of approaching You for help, even though I badly need it. Please give me the confidence to trust You with myself and to ask You for help.

T. S.

See then that you walk circumspectly, not as fools but as wise, redeeming the time, because the days are evil.
—EPH. 5:15–16

How does it make you feel when someone is late once? Twice? Three times? What if they are late all the time? I don't know where your threshold of tolerance lies; but I highly suspect that it has a lot to do with whether or not you yourself are punctual. If you are not punctual, then you usually do not expect it from another, since it makes you feel too guilty.

Why are some men always late? They start late, arrive late, and finish late. They feel that everyone has time to sit around and wait for them. Men who are not punctual usually suffer from narcissism, entitlement, or control. Narcissistic men actually believe they are more important than others, that people should wait for them with no problem. They have a need to be in control all the time, and they don't expect anyone to control their time. These men also usually overcommit themselves and cannot keep up with these schedules.

If you are not punctual, you should examine your personality carefully. You may need to realize the importance of other people's time and how waiting wastes it.

Lord, help me to respect others' time as well as my own.

L. S.

I urge you, imitate me.
—1 COR. 4:16

Every decade seems to bring a new perspective on the male gender. One decade men were to be strong; in another we were to be sensitive. Lately we are called on to be strong and sensitive. It will be interesting to see what the next classification will be. All of this labeling and qualifying is a reaction to our culture. Sadly, many men finally get comfortable with their newfound sensitivity or strength only to be asked to change and conform.

God doesn't call man to conform and change with the winds of culture but rather by following His mandates. This involves understanding our role and God's Word. As we search the Scripture we find men of incomparable strength yet uncommon love. God calls us to be men of strength and sensitivity: strong in convictions, character, and faith; sensitive to all mankind, to God's calling, to the Holy Spirit. The next time society tells us what's expected of us or who we should be, just see if this is what God would want you to do or be and whether you've been "living" it all along. If we imitate Christ, we will always be appropriate and current.

Lord, help me to conform not to the world but more and more to You.
B. D.

> *Therefore, if anyone is in Christ, he is a new creation; old things have passed away; behold, all things have become new.* —2 COR. 5:17

When I first came to Twelve-Step groups, I was never the first to talk. I remember the Thursday night I finally got the courage to go first.

Fourteen months sober, I had done my first truly honest fifth step on Wednesday night. Before I went to bed, I did the sixth and seventh steps. When I woke up on Thursday morning, something was different, almost weird. In fact, I felt so different that I was afraid I might drink again. So I asked God to help me stay sober that day before I even got out of bed.

At the meeting that night, I started the group. I had worked the seventh step, and God had really taken away my guilt—about my sexual misconduct, about the awful way I treated my family and friends, about my dishonesty and lying. He had simply taken it away!

Are you feeling guilty today? Then confess that guilt sincerely and ask God to take it away. I know He will.

God, thank You for Your perfect forgiveness when we confess our wrongdoing completely and honestly. Help me to remember that old things are passed away and all things have become new.

T. S.

In all your ways acknowledge Him,
And He shall direct your paths.
—PROV. 3:6

Bill was the epitome of social and financial success. But when I first saw him, he was sitting on his hospital bed with his head hanging down, depressed and defeated. Bill told me that he found no meaning in life anymore.

Bill had finally come to the end of his rope. In his early twenties Bill had dedicated his life to the Lord and was on the road to pursuing God's purpose for his life. Somewhere along the way Bill got caught up in earthly goals. This life detour tends to take place when we men take our eyes off God and His plan for our lives.

Does God actually have a blueprint for a man's life? Yes. Some eternal purposes apply to all men: to love God and keep His commandments; pray; love others; obey and glorify God; be a good witness; and work and provide for his family. In seeking God's specific purpose a man must consider his own physical and mental capabilities, special gifts, God-given talents, temperament, and personality.

As you follow God's general purposes, consider your constitutional endowment, and pray for God's specific will. His purpose will unfold before you.

———

Lord, show me Your purpose for my life.

L. S.

Thus says the LORD of hosts: "Consider your ways!
You have sown much, and bring in little;
You eat, but do not have enough;
You drink, but you are not filled with drink;
You clothe yourselves, but no one is warm;
And he who earns wages,
Earns wages to put into a bag with holes."
—HAG. 1:5–6

Men are looking for spiritual direction. Today there is an increase in men's awareness of their need to fill an empty part of themselves.

Robert Bly, who is a pioneer in the men's movement, has discussed the issue of father-hunger. Men are hungry for relationship with their fathers. They want to fulfill relationships they never had as boys.

However, men who pursue success, money, sex, drugs, and food to satisfy this hunger are left feeling empty, lonely, and scared.

Father-hunger can be truly filled in a relationship with God. Ask God to enter your life today, and fill the empty voids that you are facing.

———————

God, fill my empty spaces with Your love.

B. N.

*Now no chastening seems to be joyful for the
present, but grievous; nevertheless, afterward
it yields the peaceable fruit of righteousness
to those who have been trained by it.*
—HEB. 12:11

The process leading up to the seventh step is truly difficult and painful. Uprooting bad habit patterns from the past, looking at painful memories, admitting past wrongdoing, and confessing all to God, yourself, and another person are very hard to do. As the Scripture says, it is a chastening that seems grievous to us. Yet it is really the way to serenity and peace of mind, what the Scripture calls the "peaceable fruit of righteousness."

I have been with several men as they took the seventh step after they had thoroughly done the fourth, fifth, and sixth steps. They were emotionally and physically drained by honest confession. And as they did the seventh step, I saw the fruits of their labor reflected in their faces. They had the look of peaceful satisfaction, of serenity, of the "peaceable fruit of righteousness."

---

*God, thank You for Your promise of peace and serenity as a result of
being truly honest with You. I pray You will encourage me as I seek to
be honest with You.*

T. S.

> *I will instruct you and teach you in*
> *the way you should go;*
> *I will guide you with My eye.*
> —PS. 32:8

Many of the early personality theorists believed that all behavior was purposive, that every move a man made or breath he took was for a reason. According to these theorists, man is either seeking pleasure or avoiding pain at all times.

These theories of behavior are relevant to a man's understanding of recovery. Many men fail in their recovery because they lack motivation. Although one may have the tools of recovery, he also needs the motivation to use them to maintain it. Jim did great during inpatient treatment for his addiction, but one month out of treatment he had a full-blown relapse.

Jim basically had good knowledge and good intentions but lacked the motivation to apply his recovery tools at the point of relapse. Jim needed a goal that he wanted to achieve so much that he would be willing to forgo the short-term gain of the drug. Had he adopted some positive and meaningful goals early in his recovery he would have been able to work for the long-term reward.

If there is nothing meaningful or valuable waiting for a man, he will have no motivation to maintain recovery.

Lord, restore in me a pure motivation for living.

L. S.

A merry heart does good, like medicine.
—PROV. 17:22

It's no secret that in today's culture tension and anxiety are common threads in our day-to-day fabric. The fabric can only be stretched so far, though, before it frays and tears. For many of us in the past, that tension and the inability to handle it have given us all sorts of problems. Many people seek relief in alcohol, food, money, or relationships.

The world can be scary and intimidating, not to mention *serious*. How we choose to handle it will affect our emotional well-being.

We all have one tool that costs nothing and is easily accessed—laughter. You may need to go into your humor closet and blow the dust off of your laughter, but I guarantee a benefit as you approach life's valleys.

Laughter and humor have a way of chopping life's problems down to size. A man once said, "A person without humor is like a wagon without springs—jolted by every pebble." Humor and laughter act as emotional shock absorbers, not eliminating the bumps but making them easier to take.

If you want to put laughter back into your life and experience joy, I recommend studying grace. As we understand grace, then we realize our freedom to experience life at its fullest.

Lord, help me to experience the joy of my salvation in every situation.

B. D.

*Made a list of all persons we had harmed and
became willing to make amends to them all.*
—THE TWELVE STEPS OF ALCOHOLICS ANONYMOUS

*Therefore if you bring your gift to the altar, and
there remember that your brother has something
against you . . .*
—MATT. 5:23

Right now I am struggling with a relationship that has gone sour. My friend, Bill, is angry with me. And he has a right to be. I lost my temper with him, and even though my facts were correct, my delivery left much to be desired. I hurt him, and I'm truly sorry. But he won't forgive me. He can't even speak to me freely.

I've tried—I really have. I've gone to him twice, hoping to work things out. But he's still very angry with me. So here I am, left with a troubling situation. Oh, my communion with God is okay today because I have a heart of reconciliation toward Bill, but I still feel bad.

Perhaps you have a bad relationship today. If so, perhaps we can pray this prayer together:

Our Father God, please search my heart and assure me that my attitude toward _____ is right today. Please help me accept the fact that I cannot change what he thinks of me. Keep my heart from hardening against him, and make me ready to reconcile with _____ when he is ready.

T. S.

A man's pride will bring him low,
But the humble in spirit will retain honor.
—PROV. 29:23

Randy was shocked when he lost his job of five years. According to Randy it was a very easy job that required little work. He said his employer never reprimanded him, nor did he ever indicate that he would be replaced. Over the years Randy became complacent. He didn't pay attention to detail, nor did he put much effort into his job. Over a period of time Randy's complacency resulted in a decrease in production. Randy's problem was that he never thought he could be replaced.

Randy was replaced by a computer, along with a programmer to program it. Randy could not believe that he was not needed anymore, nor could he accept that a machine replaced him.

Randy is just one of many who have been replaced by high technology and by those who know how to operate the technology.

Therefore it may be important for you to continue your education to secure your job in the future. This is relative to the type of profession you're in. Some professions will never be able to automate or computerize their operations. Even if you are in a secure job, be careful that you do not forget that anyone can be replaced.

———

Lord, give me a willing spirit at work.

L. S.

> *For You have made him a little lower than the*
>   *angels,*
> *And You have crowned him with glory and honor.*
> *You have made him to have dominion over the*
>   *works of Your hands;*
> *You have put all things under his feet.*
>
> —PS. 8:5–6

One of the key issues that many men struggle with is their self-worth and identity. David seems to understand the limits of man, but also the great position given to man by God.

A man I counseled has struggled with homosexuality since he was a boy. He was sexually abused by an older brother. The shame and guilt he carried was tremendous. He felt worthless. He tried to prove that he was worthy by succeeding at his job and in church-related activities. Even so, he continued to struggle with shame about the person he was.

These verses help us recognize that God has made each one of us. We are unique and special creations of our Father. If our self-esteem could come from this vision of ourselves, we wouldn't feel so much shame and uselessness.

Lord, help me to accept the special way in which I am valued by You.

B. N.

*Love your enemies, bless those who curse you, do
good to those who hate you, and pray for those
who spitefully use you and persecute you.*
                                                    —MATT. 5:44

When I finally got around to writing an eighth-step
list, I had been around Twelve Step groups for about
two years. Most, if not all the people on my list had, in
one way or another, hurt me too. Some had hurt me
much more than I had hurt them. Why should I make
amends to them?

The reason has never been obvious to me. According to my human nature, those who hurt me should be
hurt back. It's only fair! But God's Word and the Big
Book of AA say I should love, do good, and pray for
such people. I must "clean up my side of the street."

I will never experience real serenity, real peace of
mind, if I continue to hold a grudge. Resentment, abiding anger at someone else, will shipwreck my work on
the steps if I don't free myself of it. I need to be at
peace with God and other men before I can be at
peace with myself.

---

*God, search my heart today to see if I harbor a grudge against anyone. Free me to seek that person out and make amends so that I can
have true peace of mind and communion with You.*

                                                                    T. S.

> *There is a way which seems right to a man,*
> *But its end is the way of death.*
> —PROV. 14:12

The process of recovery from any form of addiction is multidimensional. It implicates all dimensions of man's life and being. Failure to explore them may lead to relapse or an incomplete recovery program.

Men in recovery often fool themselves into believing that they can maintain recovery without making lifestyle changes. A man may need to change friends, vocation, work hours, or housing location—even separation from spouse or family of origin.

Bruce decided he didn't need to make many lifestyle changes prior to leaving the treatment program. He believed that abstinence and AA would do the trick. The treatment team advised Bruce to leave his unsuitable job; to move away from his troublemaking ex-wife; to make some new friends; and to drive home from work on the freeway rather than on happy hour row. Bruce did not heed the team recommendations and relapsed.

Bruce mistakenly believed he could get off of alcohol and then return to the very system that had adjusted to and reinforced his drinking. Had Bruce not taken risks with his recovery, his chances would have been much higher.

If a man does not learn from history, it's destined to repeat itself.

L. S.

For Christ also suffered once for sins, the just for the unjust, that He might bring us to God, being put to death in the flesh but made alive by the Spirit. —1 PETER 3:18

Like many men, I love watching those good old war movies. I especially like those set in WW II—*The Battle of the Bulge, The Dirty Dozen, The Sands of Iwo Jima.* Two of my favorites, though, are about bridges—*The Bridge of Toko Ri* and *The Bridge of Ramagan.* Both stories are based on battles that took place to preserve or destroy bridges. The bridges provided safe and secure passage for those who traveled them and were arteries for valuable supplies and nourishment to reach those on the other side.

A good bridge must have a sound structure and strength. Once on the other side, one must use the bridge as a source of supplies.

Many of us have crossed a bridge to a new life. The structure and strength of the bridge was grace, and the power that moved us was faith. On one side of the bridge we stood as sinful man, but then we saw Jesus as the bridge that brought sinful man to a holy God and the artery that supplies us and nourishes us. Trust Christ, and know that He will sustain you and that the greatest battle was won not on a bridge but on a tree, two thousand years ago.

Lord, keep me ever mindful of the new life You gave me.

B. D.

> *There is one Lawgiver, who is able to save and to destroy. Who are you to judge another?*
> —JAMES 4:12

Let's face it! Getting along with people is hard, especially for a problem person like me. Without meaning to, I become crosswise of the people in my life. The eighth step is about those damaged relationships. For if we don't square ourselves up with others, we cannot be in true communion with God.

The Scripture makes it clear: Who am I to judge another? That is God's business. My job is to judge my own conduct, to see where I have hurt others.

The hope is this: If each one of us were to just do his part, to clean up his side of the human relations street, there would be no hard feelings to create unpleasantness, no bitterness to ruin marriages, no need for counselors to heal the damage done to children.

I can do my part. Will you join me in clearing away the wreckage of the past?

God, help me not to judge anyone but myself today. Help me to make things better, in just a small way, between me and the other people in my life.

T. S.

I say then: Walk in the Spirit, and you shall not
fulfill the lust of the flesh.   —GAL. 5:16

Steve and Wanda had been married for three years prior to coming for counseling. Their primary complaint was sexual. Wanda felt that Steve rarely wanted to have sex with her. Steve said that he had experienced a decrease in his desire to have sex with Wanda over the past three years.

Steve was having a secret affair with someone—not with another woman, but with himself. Steve had a problem with compulsive masturbation. Steve had masturbated when he was single and thought that he would leave the habit behind when he married. He surprisingly discovered that masturbation was also useful in marriage. He could still have pleasure when Wanda didn't feel like having sex. By masturbating Steve did not have to worry about being sexually frustrated at night. Steve also discovered that masturbation was less exhausting than making love and took less time. Avoiding intercourse also enabled Steve to avoid his fears of failure and performance in lovemaking.

In therapy Steve had to come to the realization that his habit was keeping him and his wife from experiencing the sexual oneness which God had designed for them in marriage. He also had to deal with his performance anxiety and fear of intimacy.

Lord, instill in me a right spirit about sexual intimacy in my
marriage.

L. S.

> *Six days you shall labor and do all your work, but the seventh day is the Sabbath of the LORD your God. In it you shall do no work: you, nor your son, nor your daughter, nor your manservant, nor your maidservant, nor your cattle, nor your stranger who is within your gates.*
>
> —EX. 20:9–10

As we try to lead our families in spiritual issues, it is important to recognize the need for spiritual reflection. God commands us to keep the Sabbath holy. Recovery involves spiritual reflection and relying on God for strength. We have a weekly need to rest from work and to reflect on spiritual issues.

Many men today are addicted to work. At work they find all their sense of self-worth and success. Many men work on Sundays, not taking time to meet their own spiritual needs or to be examples for their families.

Men need to face two important issues in the passage. One is the need for spiritual reflection. The other is the need for rest from work. Do you take time off and time for spiritual reflection?

God, help me to see my need for spiritual growth and to honor that by keeping Your day holy.

B. N.

*In whatever you judge another you condemn
yourself; for you who judge practice the
same things.*   —ROM. 2:1

I had just come home from a night out with friends, and Mike, my roommate, was giving me my messages. He was in bed, but obviously not asleep, and his tone was angry. When I asked him if something was wrong, he said, "No."

The next morning we talked about it. I had been ill, and Mike knew I had started a new medication with potentially serious side effects. When I didn't come home or call, Mike got worried. He thought I might be sick somewhere, with no one to help me. Mike pointed out that I had been inconsiderate of him for not letting him know where I was and that I was okay. He was right, and I apologized.

I can hurt people without trying. Quite frankly, my ongoing struggle with poor self-esteem causes me to forget that someone might care about me. So I can hurt him . . . by accident. And those people need to be on my eighth-step list as much as the people I tried to hurt on purpose.

Lord, let me remember the people who love me when I write my amends list. Loving someone like me is often hurtful.

T. S.

> *Do not deprive one another except with consent for*
> *a time, that you may give yourselves to fasting and*
> *prayer; and come together again so that Satan does*
> *not tempt you because of your lack of self-control.*
> —1 COR. 7:5

Incest is one of the most tragic events that can occur in a family. It can occur at every level of society. It can occur in any family if the conditions are right. When one person in a family is not fulfilling his or her pre-scribed role, then someone else in the family will.

Incest usually occurs under five conditions. First, there must be an emotional connection with the vic-tim. Second, the wife must not be meeting the father's emotional or sexual needs. Third, there must be a time where the father and the victim are alone. Fourth, the father must overcome his own guilt and inhibitions. Fifth, he must overcome any resistance from the vic-tim.

Incest occurs most often when one's daughter is forced to play an adult spousal role. This usually oc-curs when couples stay together and never resolve their marital problems. If you are a man and have daughters, be sure that you and your wife truly love each other and meet each other's needs.

See to it that your wife meets your needs; then no one else will have to.

L. S.

As for me, I will walk in my integrity.
—PS. 26:11

I have heard it said that the true test of a man's character is not in how he conducts himself in public but in how he conducts himself in private. It's easy to mask yourself and conduct yourself properly when multitudes are watching; the test comes when we're alone. In the privacy of our homes, offices, and minds, are we more lax in our behavior? Do we compromise our values? Are we genuinely humble when the spotlight is off?

Another saying states that "the measure of a man's character is what he would do if he knew he would never be found out."

In Hebrew the word *integrity* means unimpaired, or wholeness. With this in mind we must ask ourselves what impairs us from being wholesome and pure, what keeps us from experiencing Christlikeness wholly and holy.

As we recognize those things, we can confess and remove them, starting fresh in public as well as in private. God does not place a premium on human values but instead on a heart that is deep in spirit, commitment, honesty, and humility.

Father, guide me in honesty, strengthen me in commitment, cover me with the truth.

B. D.

> *Bless those who persecute you; bless and do*
> *not curse.*
> —ROM. 12:14

After I came to Twelve Step meetings, it took me two solid years to write an eighth-step list. When I finally got around to it, my egotism, one of my most troublesome and abiding character defects, got in the way. I wrote almost forty names of people I was sure I had hurt significantly. Some of them were people I hardly knew, but I knew I had caused them serious, ongoing harm. Thank God, my sponsor came to my rescue.

He pointed out that I was not as powerful as I thought and that other people are not as sensitive as I am. Many are capable of just shrugging off the nasty tidbits I sometimes pass out.

As he and I went over my list, we deleted a cousin of mine who, when we were playing kids' games, I thought I had hurt. We also removed bartenders, people who hung out in bars, and nameless people who had witnessed my rude behavior. After we accounted for my egotism, there were twenty-six people on my list—twenty-six people whom I had really hurt and to whom I should make amends.

Lord, protect me from my egotism when I judge my effect on other people. Help me to see myself objectively—as I really am.

T. S.

The fear of man brings a snare,
But whoever trusts in the LORD
shall be safe.

—PROV. 29:25

It's difficult to be assertive in the workplace. So we conceal our anger at work and then take it out on those who are closest to us.

Assertiveness is the act of sharing one's feelings or needs to a significant other as they arise. Assertiveness brings a decrease in anxiety and an increase in happiness. Concealment brings an increase in anxiety and a decrease in happiness.

Most of us fail to be assertive at work because we don't want to lose our jobs. Truth is sacrificed for the job itself. If we have a beef, we may bite our upper lip. In addition, some of us want to appear easygoing and adaptive so that our superiors will perceive us as team players. Some of us have even become "yes men" for the sake of some menial promotions.

By failing to assert our rights, thoughts, feelings, and needs, we men tend to lose self-respect. An employer may not throw a ticker tape parade for you when you speak out, but he can only have respect for the man who is his own man. Jesus was assertive in His own way and is a good example to examine as you face your own small world.

Others will only respect you to the degree which you respect yourself.

L. S.

> *Do not labor for the food which perishes, but for*
> *the food which endures to everlasting life, which*
> *the Son of Man will give you, because God the*
> *Father has set His seal on Him.* —JOHN 6:27

One of the masculine identity issues is the need to find a way to make an impact on the world. Most men feel that the best or easiest way to make this impact is through their work. God encourages us to work for food that endures to eternity. The kind of food he speaks of here is not that which usually comes from work. It is the food that is found in the Bible.

A man who had become very successful in business found himself in a deep depression. He had won fame in his profession and could easily retire with the income that he was generating. He realized that the perishable food was not enough to feed his hunger. He began a relationship with God and started experiencing a joy he had never known before.

What kind of hunger are you trying to fill today? Are you sure you are taking in the right food to nourish you?

———————

God, feed me with the food that will last through eternity.

B. N.

*But when you do good and suffer for it, if you take
it patiently, this is commendable before God.*
—1 PETER 2:20

After I attended Twelve-Step groups for two years, I
entered into a partnership in the musical instrument
business. But it didn't work out, and after six months
we dissolved the partnership.

I lost a substantial amount of money. "We both made
mistakes," I told myself, "but I've forgiven him his mistakes and he, mine. I certainly don't owe him any
amends."

Many months later we met again when he walked
into a restaurant where I was eating. I became so angry when I saw him that I left. And I stayed angry.

I knew I had to clean up my side of the street. I
phoned him, and we met for coffee. "Ken," I said, "I'm
sorry for my mistakes. I used poor judgment and
should have known better."

"You're right!" he said. "It's about time you admitted it!"

At first I was angry, but then I realized it didn't matter. I was free of guilt and resentment.

*God, thank You for freeing me of guilt and resentment when I clean
up my side of the street.*

T. S.

> *Draw near to God and He will draw near to you.*
> *Cleanse your hands, you sinners; and purify your*
> *hearts, you double-minded.* —JAMES 4:8

A man's sexual thoughts are hidden deep in the secret canals of his mind, far from the awareness of those around him.

Men are instinctively ashamed of their sexual desire. Maintaining a secret sexual thought life feeds this deep shame. This cesspool of shame grows deeper with every secret thought.

Do you harbor thoughts that you feel you must hide? If your most secret thoughts were revealed to those who supposedly know you, would you be embarrassed? If the answer is yes, you are struggling with a dilemma.

We can drain some of the shame out of this pool within us by deciding to regain some control over our secret thought lives. We can have some victory over this problem by deciding to concentrate on things that are pure, by being more transparent with other men about our temptations, and by seeking the mind of Christ.

_____

God, help me to have pure thoughts today and to be transparent with others.

L. S.

Put on the whole armor of God.
—EPH. 6:11

My father was a soldier. He was in two wars, Korea and Vietnam. The few times that my father spoke about his experiences he named three things critical to survival in battle. Number one, he said, was a good leader. Number two was effective weapons, and number three was protection.

Chances are I will never go to battle as he did, but I've realized that in this world a war is definitely raging—a spiritual war between Satan and believers. My father's three things are just as critical and relevant in this war. We need a leader, and we have one in God the Father. Our weaponry is our faith, and our protection is the armor He has given us.

A careful look at Ephesians 6:11–18 confirms that God our "leader" has given us seven primary things to secure us in the battle:

1. Truth
2. Righteousness
3. The gospel
4. Faith
5. Salvation
6. God's Word
7. Prayer

Father, may I put on my whole armor daily to be an effective soldier for Christ.

B. D.

> Made direct amends to such people wherever
> possible, except when to do so would injure
> them or others.
>   —THE TWELVE STEPS OF ALCOHOLICS ANONYMOUS

> "If your enemy hungers, feed him.
> If he thirsts, give him a drink;
> For in so doing you will heap
>   coals of fire on his head."
> Do not be overcome by evil, but
> overcome evil with good.
>   —ROM. 12:20–21

My friend, Jim, and I have had a falling out. That's not necessarily unusual among recovering addicts; we are, after all, problem people. What is unusual is that we haven't made up. Jim will not forgive me.

I've gone to him twice in the spirit of the ninth step. Nothing has changed. But my biggest problem has been in overcoming evil with good. I have struggled to be civil. Since we work for the same organization, I see him often. He is always quiet and sullen when I'm around. That makes me angry and I want to strike back. But as God allows me, I have tried to be civil to him.

I think it's working. I don't know if it's having an effect on Jim, but I'm not as angry with him as I was. Slowly I'm getting off the hook of my resentment. I thank God that I can take the right path, as the ninth step says, of love and forgiveness.

God, thank You for Your hard words regarding resentment against our brothers. I pray I will be faithful to the spirit of the ninth step.

                                        T. S.

*Then, when desire has conceived, it gives birth
to sin; and sin, when it is full-grown, brings
forth death.*
                                      —JAMES 1:15

Sam entered the sexual addictions group by court order. He had been arrested for soliciting a prostitute
and escaped jail by agreeing to seek therapy. Sam first
solicited a prostitute years ago on an out-of-town business trip. He was certain that it would only be a one-
time thing since he was happily married with three
children. Instead this experience was only the first of
hundreds of encounters.

During the first five years of Sam's addiction, he
only acted out while out of town on business. Then the
three years prior to being arrested, Sam started frequenting prostitutes in his hometown—risky, but more
exciting.

Like Sam, most sex addicts don't intend to become
sex addicts. Most start out by simple experimentation,
followed by rationalization, and then compulsion,
needing more of the experience to get the same effect.
And the more risky the acting out, the greater the
high. Finally, most sex addicts stop being careful after
a while and end up being found out. If you can identify
with Sam even moderately, it is likely that you are a
sexual addict.

_____

Seek help—break the cycle before the cycle breaks you.

                                                    L. S.

> *I am persuaded that neither death nor life, nor*
> *angels nor principalities nor powers, nor things*
> *present nor things to come, nor height nor depth,*
> *nor any other created thing, shall be able to*
> *separate us from the love of God which is in*
> *Christ Jesus our Lord.*
> —ROM. 8:38–39

While working on recovery issues, men often worry that they have been rejected by God. Many times the issues that bring men to recovery are sins. This can leave them feeling isolated and alone. This loneliness often leads them to search for God and to reconcile with Him.

A man came to my office and stated that God had rejected him. I asked him how he knew that. He told me that he had committed adultery and felt that God could never love or forgive him after he had done something like that. We discussed these verses, and he was able to see that even though we do sin, God still loves us. It was essential for this man to break off this affair and recognize it as sin, but he also needed the reassurance that God could love him and forgive him in spite of his sin.

God loves us. When we really connect with that love, it gives us more strength and motivation to flee sin.

God, help me recognize that Your love is never ending.

B. N.

*As we have opportunity, let us do good to all,
especially to those who are of the household
of faith.*
—GAL. 6:10

Norbert and Blanche were my parents' next-door neighbors and good friends. But in 1970, I had a big argument with them and refused to speak to them.

When I moved to Chicago, I left all those old resentments behind me in New York. What a relief—or so I thought. When I got to Twelve-Step groups, however, it was obvious that I owed them all amends. But, I thought, they're so far away. What's the difference if I'm never going to see them again?

One day, when I was having a bad time of it, none of the AA magic was working. I realized that I had let many amends go undone. I wrote to Norbert and Blanche, apologizing and asking them to forgive me. Several weeks later, they called me. We chatted pleasantly about old times. Then they said they loved me!

I never spoke to Norbert again. He died of cancer within the year. Thank God for that last conversation with my friend Norbert, who loved me.

God, thank You for softening an old heart like mine. I pray that You will remind all of us of the urgency for amends.

T. S.

> *Watch and pray, lest you enter into temptation. The*
> *spirit indeed is willing, but the flesh is weak.*
> —MATT. 26:41

It is important to understand the dynamics of male sexuality when talking about masturbation. Men have two basic sexual needs, the biological and the psychological. The biological need is met first, then the psychological. With women this process is reversed. Men need to know that they were desired and that they pleased their mate.

Why is this understanding so important? Masturbation only meets the biological need and not the psychological. Thus when one masturbates he feels that he is satisfied when actually he isn't. This is part of the reason why he must continue to masturbate so often. He is driven to feed the psychological through the physical, but doesn't realize it. The only sure thing that is accomplished through this vicious cycle is the production of shame.

Thus, it is only through having sex with the wife that God has blessed us with that our physical and psychological sexual needs can be met. Compulsive or even occasional masturbation is only putting a Band-Aid™ on a deeper problem. Sex is transgenital, and we men must look beyond our own bodies for true satisfaction.

Lord, show me the way to deeper sexual fulfillment.

L. S.

*Do you not know that those who run in a race all
run, but one receives the prize? Run in such a way
that you may obtain it.* —1 COR. 9:24

Some people seem to live a healthy Christian life. Things are even and balanced, with priorities intact. They seem to negotiate life's hurdles without breaking their stride. Sometimes they don't even appear winded. How do they do it?

Fitness experts agree that regular exercise increases one's energy level. The runner who trains consistently is always ready for the race. Similarly, the child of God who trains regularly in prayer, meditation, and Bible study has more energy for Christlikeness, vitality for the gospel, and zest for walking and talking the Christian life.

Training is essential. The person who is in shape and knows the course is equipped with stamina and confidence. Attitude, however, may separate those who merely run the race from those who run to win. The Christian's attitude is shaped by his relationship with Christ. By grace we are free from the tyranny of the law.

As we are freed from encumbrances that so easily entangle us (Heb. 12:1), we have space to stride, room to stretch out, and freedom to live.

Father, strengthen me so that I might run life's race with endurance.
B. D.

> *Leave your gift there before the altar, and go your way. First be reconciled to your brother, and then come and offer your gift.* —MATT. 5:24

David was the one who first discovered that I was an alcoholic. He got me into treatment. Even though I worked for him for two years after I got sober, I never really made amends. And it bothered me.

One day, when I couldn't stand it anymore, I called him and we met for lunch. I told him that I knew I had hurt him when he discovered I was a closet drunk. I knew that I had caused him great problems. I told him I was sorry and asked him to forgive me. I also told him I appreciated his help and his friendship.

Tears came to David's eyes. No matter how self-sufficient, how self-reliant a man is, he can always benefit from an honest apology, sincerely meant.

I seldom see David these days. We travel in different circles. But we'll always be friends.

God, thank You for using my conscience to keep me honest so that I can continue to be reconciled with my brothers and with You.

T. S.

Put on the Lord Jesus Christ, and make no
provision for the flesh, to fulfill its lusts.
—ROM. 13:14

What does the Bible say about masturbation? Very little. Those who say that masturbation is a sin use Matthew 5:27–30 as their proof, saying that lusting in the heart is the same thing as committing adultery. This is true, of course.

Can one masturbate and yet not sin? The answer is yes, if one can masturbate without fantasizing. The physical act of stimulating oneself is not the main problem but the thoughts that accompany the act. Have you ever tried to masturbate without fantasizing? It is next to impossible because the male sexual response is tied into a visual sensory experience. Most men must see something stimulating or imagine something to get aroused. Herein lies the problem of masturbation for the single male. He cannot fantasize about a wife. Therefore his fantasy life would obviously center around someone else. This is where the sin is born along with the ensuing guilt and shame.

If you are a single male, you are likely struggling with masturbation. It is important for you to remember that your physical sexual desires are God-given, natural, and all right. They become destructive only when they are not controlled and are allowed to run free.

Lord, help me to delay sexual gratification.

L. S.

> *These things I have spoken to you, that in Me you may have peace. In the world you will have tribulation; but be of good cheer, I have overcome the world.*
> —JOHN 16:33

It often seems that evil is winning in the world. The evil seems overpowering as we struggle with the issues related to recovery. At times we feel powerless and out of control. God warns us that we will have trouble but assures us that He has overcome the world.

A man named Paul recently attended a support meeting. There he was faced with a situation that he did not know how to handle. A man at the support group had lost his wife and children and was threatening to take his own life. As the man described his plight, Paul recognized the man's pain. Paul had also lost his family. He was able to share his experience, and by the end of the group the man agreed not to take his life.

There certainly will be bleak days as we journey on this earth. But there is a way to get through the pain and have peace in spite of our circumstances.

Lord, remind me today that the victory over this world has been won by You.

B. N.

*. . . being filled with the fruits of righteousness
which are by Jesus Christ, to the glory and praise
of God.* —PHIL. 1:9–11

My sister is fifteen years older than I. She has always
been more like a second mother than a sister. She loves
me very much. I learned to use her love for me against
her. Whenever I wanted something, I knew Alice
would get it for me if she could.

Truth to tell, I didn't love her. I was incapable of loving anyone, including myself. My idea of love was to
make it pay. And it surely did with Alice.

After I got to Twelve Step meetings, I realized I
owed Alice a big amends. My sponsor assured me I
needed to tell her the truth.

One evening when she called me, I made my
amends, leaving nothing out. She ended the call
quickly and didn't call back for a week. I thought I had
lost a sister.

When she did call, she said, "I want you to know that
everything is okay."

When Alice had cancer surgery three years ago, you
can bet I was at her bedside when she woke up. I love
her very much.

---

*God, thank You for putting love in my heart. Continue to give me a
sensitive conscience so I can continue to glorify You.*

T. S.

> *And you shall know the truth, and the truth shall*
> *make you free.*
> —JOHN 8:32

Ron entered treatment at age thirty-five. He was severely depressed and had tried to take his life. He also had some severe drinking and marital problems. As I counseled Ron, I began to explore his life experiences. Ron said that he had always felt like there was something wrong with him, that maybe he was inferior. These feelings, of course, severely affected Ron's relationships. When the pain got too bad for Ron to handle he turned to alcohol to numb the pain.

I suspected that Ron had been abused as a child, either mentally or sexually, because of the shame in Ron's thoughts and feelings. As I asked Ron if he had ever been sexually abused, he broke down crying, holding his head down in shame but relief. He said, "Since I was a little boy, no one has ever asked me that question."

Ron's problem is common among male sexual abuse victims. Over 90 percent of all male sexual abuse victims never tell anyone about it. Ron was fortunate; he was able to reveal the secret.

If you are an adult male and you have been sexually abused, you no longer have to keep the secret. The only way to break the inner shame cycle is to tell someone what happened to you.

The only freedom from your pain will come by breaking the secrecy chain.

L. S.

> *Brethren, if a man is overtaken in any trespass, you*
> *who are spiritual restore such a one in a spirit of*
> *gentleness, considering yourself lest you also be*
> *tempted.*   —GAL. 6:1

David was writhing in pain. He never saw the offender coming. The impact was violent. David lay there with a separated shoulder. He looked helpless. It was as if his tears cried out, "Please help—it hurts so bad." Moments later the trainer got there, followed by a doctor. They would do what was necessary to help David. With compassion they let David know it would be all right. However, the hard part was in setting the shoulder. David knew the intensity of the pain but felt secure that these men would put him on his feet again. It couldn't be just anyone to help David; it would take special men with strength, compassion, gentleness, and knowledge.

So often we fall or know another who has fallen. The most difficult thing is getting back up. When we can't pick ourselves up and ask for help, a strong and gentle brother can lift us up. The word *restore* can mean putting a dislocated limb into place or bringing behavior back into line. Either way, gentleness and love are required.

Are you in pain or have you fallen out of line? Maybe you know someone that is. You may need a brother or you may be the brother that resets the bone and puts it back in line.

As you look at one who has fallen, look at yourself as one who can help.

B. D.

> *Therefore, as the elect of God, holy and beloved,*
> *put on tender mercies, kindness, humbleness of*
> *mind, meekness, long-suffering; bearing with one*
> *another, and forgiving one another, if anyone has a*
> *complaint against another; even as Christ forgave*
> *you, so you also must do.*   —COL. 3:12–13

My friend Bill says that if he feels good going to do an amends, he's doing it wrong. He means that if he is very honest about what he has done wrong, he is emotionally involved.

I echo Bill's statement. If I am truly sorry for harm done and must face the person, I get anxious. I am both humiliated at admitting my wrongs and apprehensive because I don't know how my amends will be received. Yet I cannot live either well or long if I don't make restitution.

But amends are almost always received graciously. Most of my amends were to friends or working acquaintances who liked me. When I came to make amends, they were pleased that my life was better and that our relationship had taken a better turn.

God, thank You for the courage to make amends for past harm done. Continue to encourage me as I make things right with my fellows.

T. S.

For I wish that all men were even as I myself. But each one has his own gift from God, one in this manner and another in that. —1 COR. 7:7

Single males are often considered defective by many in our society. A male in his late twenties or thirties who is not married and not in school may be accused of being gay or odd. He may also be labeled a narcissist or playboy. The fact is, though, there is nothing wrong with being single. Marriage is not for everyone.

There are both assets and liabilities to remaining single. In 1 Corinthians 7 the apostle Paul specifically states that those who have the gift of celibacy can remain single and those who do not should marry rather than burn with sexual desire.

What does this mean for today's single male? Very simply, if you feel you have the gift of celibacy and do not struggle with sexual desire or loneliness, then remain single if you choose, and continue to serve God. If you feel you are not endowed with this gift, then sustain moral purity until you find the woman God wants you to marry.

Finally, to remain single and celibate is better than to marry under social pressure or for the wrong reasons. You may be struggling very hard with this dilemma, but God will give you the patience and control that you need until His will for your life is revealed.

Remember that some of the greatest men who have walked the earth have been single.

L. S.

> *If we say that we have no sin, we deceive ourselves,*
> *and the truth is not in us.* —1 JOHN 1:8

Sometimes men can deceive themselves and believe that they're always right. It's hard for many men to admit that they're wrong. Men have a need to feel adequate and not show weakness. Somehow, they see admitting wrong as a sign of weakness. This sets them up to be deceitful and self-protective.

When Jim and Janet were in marital counseling, one of the issues that affected their marriage was Jim's compulsive lying. He was a Christian and would feel convicted about his lies and confess them later, but he continued to lie. When asked why he lied, he stated that he didn't like looking bad in front of other people.

All of us have fallen short of God's perfect mark. It is better to face the truth that we are not perfect and allow others to see that in us than to lie or be self-protective to cover up the truth.

God, help me to see my weaknesses and shortcomings, and strengthen me to address them head on.

B. N.

> *Pursue peace with all men, and holiness, without*
> *which no one will see the Lord . . . lest any root of*
> *bitterness springing up cause trouble, and by this*
> *many become defiled.* —HEB. 12:14–15

Leon's nickname was Mr. Resentment. Always angry, never satisfied, Leon attended Twelve Step meetings for years, always complaining about his employer. If I spoke to him about making amends or freeing himself from resentment, Leon exploded in torrents of bitterness against just about everybody. Needless to say, I did not often seek his company.

I spoke to Leon just before Christmas. He had been working for the post office for two months and asked me if I thought he should ask for a raise. I suggested he wait a while. Leon was not pleased.

Two weeks later I heard that Leon was dead. He rented a cheap hotel room in Chicago, got drunk, and shot himself in the head.

There are many like Leon, who cannot or will not give up their bitterness. Many of them end up the way Leon did. The rest live pitifully purposeless lives.

Lord, thank You that I can see bitterness for the poison it is. If I can help, lead me to someone like Leon with the good news of Your peace and love.

T. S.

These things I have spoken to you, that in Me you may have peace. In the world you will have tribulation; but be of good cheer, I have overcome the world.
—JOHN 16:33

Being stuck at a job or a job position where you are unhappy is trying. Going to work every day seems like a major task. A man who is stuck at his job cannot wait till the day ends. He spends most of his time resenting his job, himself, and work in general. He feels hopeless. As he watches others around him move up and achieve success, he begins to resent them. He usually ends up quitting the job and waiting till another one comes his way.

Why might a man get stuck at a career level? Sometimes he is simply in a dead-end job. No matter what he does, he cannot move up. Sometimes people can keep a man from moving up, particularly people who want all the action to themselves. A man also may be stuck vocationally because of personality, limited skills, the need for more education, poor leadership skills, or lack of personal initiative and ambition.

If you feel that you are in this vocational dilemma, examine your work environment, skills, personality, and initiative.

Lord, show me my strengths and weaknesses as they relate to my career goals.

L. S.

*And no wonder! For Satan himself transforms
himself into an angel of light.* —2 COR. 11:14

Deception. The sound of this word brings images of shrouded beings that are up to no good. Deception clothes itself in many ways. It can appeal to our senses and better judgment, and always sound so true. Deception can be anything it wants to be—beautiful, logical, prosperous. Too often, however, this multipronged fork pokes, prods, and finally embeds itself into a heart.

Every day we are confronted by immorality, clouded ethics, greed, and violence. Most of these are blatant, but others knock on our doors subtly. As our mind opens its door, it may only see the surface of an inviting presence, never knowing what lies below or behind. Many times it happens quickly and without warning. But the deceiver has thought it out well. He has a plan. Taken in by a flash. No pain, no outward scars. Upon realizing our dilemma, we feel the internal bleeding and then feel the pain. *Deceived.*

There is help, however. The believer who incorporates God's truth in his life has the weapon necessary to protect himself.

Father, I pray for discernment and awareness. Help me to see deception clearly before it causes pain.

B. D.

*But the wisdom that is from above is first pure,
then peaceable, gentle, willing to yield, full of
mercy and good fruits, without partiality and
without hypocrisy.*
                                    —JAMES 3:17–18

David and I were discussing why prayer is preached about so little. David came to this conclusion: Prayer is so ineffective in the lives of men because men don't pray.

Is that true? Do we say "I'll pray about it" the same way we greet people with "How are you?" when we really don't care? Do we say we pray more often than we pray? I think so.

If we are to do our best with the ninth step, we must pray for knowledge from above and for willingness to yield. And we must avoid hypocrisy.

Hypocrisy slips in when we try to do amends too quickly, in a hurry to "Get it all behind us." We must be careful to pray about each amends, seeking the counsel of others so that we can make amends that are appropriate, well thought out, and sincere. We must be men of prayer when we make amends.

---

*God, thank You for the wisdom You provide from above. I pray You
will encourage me to pray hard over each amends before I do it.*

                                                        T. S.

> *Servants, be submissive to your masters with all fear, not only to the good and gentle, but also to the harsh.*
> **—1 PETER 2:18**

Some men cannot keep a regular job because they cannot work for anyone. They always end up getting fired or getting into an argument with the boss. No matter how nice the boss is, he's always unreasonable and always unfair. For men who cannot deal with authority, life is but a series of new and old jobs.

A man who cannot deal with authority will usually go out and try to start his own business, thinking that will somehow be the answer to his job dilemma. Eventually, he ends up losing the business because he cannot deal with customers or employees. His need to be in control and to be right ultimately blocks all goals for a successful career.

The Bible is very clear that as men we are to submit to those in authority over us. When we fail to do so, serious consequences happen to us. These consequences can serve to create further resentment toward authority figures. If you struggle with submitting to authority, you need to quit fighting and turn your will over to God. He would be a good boss to start with. If you don't want to submit, then be prepared to resent work till the day you retire.

Lord, help me to control my independent spirit.

L. S.

> *. . . looking diligently lest anyone fall short of the grace of God; lest any root of bitterness springing up cause trouble, and by this many become defiled.*
> —HEB. 12:15

Bitterness about past issues can hinder the recovery process. I worked with a man named Steve who had a lot of bitterness toward his father. While Steve was growing up, his father stated that Steve would never amount to anything. He also said that Steve wasn't worth the gunpowder it would take to blow his brains out.

Steve went on to graduate from medical school. As he walked across the stage after receiving his diploma, he turned to his father in the audience and shook the diploma at him. He cursed him and stated that he *was* worth something. His attitude was, "See, Dad! I showed you." Six years later, however, Steve was in the hospital struggling with drug addiction and marriage problems. The bitterness Steve held against his father was ruining him and his family.

Don't underestimate the power of bitterness to destroy lives. Learn how to resolve your anger toward others without letting it sour in your soul.

God, help me to resolve my anger so that it does not turn bitter.

B. N.

My little children, let us not love in word or in tongue, but in deed and in truth.
—1 JOHN 3:18

When people come to Twelve Step meetings, they are usually in a hurry to do all twelve steps and graduate. That's why we say, "There is no graduation." Even so, most of us still try to rush through.

Often that mistake is made with the ninth step. Feeling guilty and uncomfortable and seeking relief, we often rush in without much thought or preparation. We want to settle back down to business as usual. And the amends often go badly. How often have people who love us and whom we have hurt heard us say, "I'm sorry, I'll never do that again! " only to have us do it again? Promises and apologies, without our living out our amends, are no amends at all.

We must first understand exactly what harm we have done. Then we must make the correct amends. We will always need the help of a sponsor or an understanding friend. Finally, we approach the person we have harmed—with an excellent chance that the amends will be accepted with good grace and understanding.

God, help me to be patient with the ninth step. Provide the right person to help me check out and plan my amends.

T. S.

> *Let us therefore come boldly to the throne of grace,*
> *that we may obtain mercy and find grace to help in*
> *time of need.*
> —HEB. 4:16

One problem that all men face is dealing with emotions. Most of us would probably prefer just to do away with emotions so we wouldn't have to work so hard at trying to deal with them. As young boys most of us were told that we were not supposed to be emotional. Yet emotions continue to surface in our lives, day by day and minute by minute.

For the man who struggles with an addictive personality, emotions may create severe problems. He is terrified by some emotions, particularly fear, anxiety, anger, loneliness, and love. To him they are an alarm that warns to escape or flee. He runs from them, represses them, or projects them onto others.

The man in recovery uses his emotions as radar to tell him when something is wrong. When this man first experiences an emotion, he identifies it and tells himself that it is okay to have it. If he can't process the emotion effectively and determine the inner need, he humbly asks God and someone else for help. Finally, he views his emotions as God's gift to be used for his good.

A man cannot change his feelings, only his response to them.

L. S.

For as he thinks in his heart, so is he.
—PROV. 23:7

We often speak of discernment as it relates to specific choices we make. Usually when we are unclear on a particular decision, discernment is that tool that weighs the evidence and brings clarity to thought. This can be of great value when we come in contact with people. And God has given us an extra hand when it comes to discernment with others. Many people are their own undoing. In a social or professional setting we can frequently "discern" the "fiber" of a man by his conversation and thoughts. I have heard it said that a man's words are a path to his heart. The inference is that if we could use his words as stones and follow them one by one, we could see what kind of condition his heart is in, not to mention where it lives. The heart's condition and where it lives are indicators of priorities—heavenly or earthly.

If someone were to take your thoughts and words and trace them back to your heart, what would he find? Would he find a home with a firm foundation supported by beams of God's Word, or would he find a loose, temporary structure swaying with every wind of change?

_____

Father, make my heart pure and my thoughts a reflection of You.

B. D.

> *Continued to take personal inventory and when we were wrong promptly admitted it.*
> —THE TWELVE STEPS OF ALCOHOLICS ANONYMOUS

> *. . . to everyone who is among you, not to think of himself more highly than he ought to think, but to think soberly, as God has dealt to each one a measure of faith.*
> —ROM. 12:3

When I first began to take moral inventory, I was confused. There were several how-to books around, so many in fact that the differing opinions about what should and should not be included in an inventory made me even more confused.

Some of the books suggested that we make sure to look at our good qualities. Unfortunately, when I started taking inventory, I didn't think I had any good qualities. And the Scripture suggests that thinking too highly of ourselves is dangerous. Instead, we should take inventory of our character defects.

Through my experience with taking inventory, I have learned to look at my guilt, resentments, anger, and self-pity—G-R-A-S-P. All the other defects will become apparent when I look for the fearsome foursome. I will find out about my positive inventory items from other people as they see me grow and change.

God, help me to look at my defects honestly, without prejudice. Help me to find the GRASP in my life and dig it out.

T. S.

*Therefore humble yourselves under the mighty
hand of God, that He may exalt you in due time,
casting all your care upon Him, for He cares
for you.*   —1 PETER 5:6–7

One of the most important steps in Twelve Step recovery is number ten. The recovering person is encouraged to maintain a daily inventory. This step is strategically important to the daily progress of a man's recovery for two main reasons. First, Step 10 is the brother to Step 4, which calls for the initial inventory of the defects in a man's life. Secondly, Step 10 ensures that a man's old defects don't return.

A man who is truly in positive recovery maintains a daily inventory of his behavior, feelings, thoughts, relationships, and personality. He maintains a radar system to seek out trouble spots. For example, one of my character defects is control. When I unwittingly get into a control mode, my radar picks up on it and warns me. I in turn identify what I'm trying to control and then make the decision to let go.

The daily inventory fosters a low-stress, low-anxiety healing environment for recovery one day at a time. A man's daily inventory enables him to make sure that problems or feelings from one day do not go into the next day.

A man in recovery does not find today's problems in tomorrow.

L. S.

Whenever you stand praying, if you have anything against anyone, forgive him, that your Father in heaven may also forgive you your trespasses.
—MARK 11:25

It is often hard to understand what forgiveness really is. Walter Wangerin has defined it as a "divine absurdity." Forgiveness is essential if we are to have a relationship with Christ. We must be willing to forgive others or Christ will not forgive us.

A man named Pete once came in for counseling. He was struggling with a lot of anger toward an uncle. When he was a boy, the uncle had sexually abused him and had left many emotional scars. Pete had never worked through the anger or grief of the abuse. For Pete forgiveness was out of the question. Once he was able to work through the anger and grieve the loss of innocence, Pete was able to begin the process of forgiveness. God hates the sin of sexual abuse more than we do. Pete came to see that God forgives the sinner and still hates the sin.

Pete needed to forgive his uncle for his own sake. Unforgiveness and bitterness was destroying Pete and still gave his uncle power over him. Forgiveness brings healing to the soul.

God, uncover any unforgiveness in my heart, and strengthen me with the power to forgive.

B. N.

*The soul of Jonathan was knit to the soul of David,
and Jonathan loved him as his own soul.*
—1 SAM. 18:1

Men need friends. Many men don't have a close friend, but I hope that as part of your recovery you will try to develop closer men friends. The friendship between Jonathan and David was soul to soul. There was nothing unmasculine or immoral about their love for each other. They were truly brothers who wanted to see the best happen for each other.

When I reflect on my friends, I think of a few who fit that description. One is named Benny. He and I grew up together in high school. His friendship is one of the best I have ever known. Though we have been separated by many miles for several years, we still experience each other as kindred spirits whenever we talk or get together. He is a friend who really knows and understands me, yet loves and accepts me anyway.

Do you have a friend like that? If you don't, begin to ask God to send a man into your life to befriend.

Lord, help me to establish true friendships that bring glory and honor to You.

B. N.

> *Stand fast therefore in the liberty by which Christ*
> *has made us free, and do not be entangled again*
> *with a yoke of bondage.*
> —GAL. 5:1

If Christ has made us free indeed, why do we walk around so heavily burdened by guilt?

My dictionary says *guilt* is "the feeling that one is to blame." And feelings are not facts. It is possible to feel guilty without really being guilty. There are two kinds of guilt: true guilt and false guilt.

Many of us experience huge amounts of false guilt. We have been conditioned by others to be manipulated by guilty feelings even when we've done nothing wrong. A simple sigh, a raised eyebrow, or a stern look can cause us to believe that we're wrong when we're not. This kind of guilt needs to be written in our inventory so we can see it for the lie it is. When we're free of false guilt, we can take a good look at our true guilt. We need to speak with someone else experienced in discerning true from false guilt. We cannot do it on our own.

God, thank You for telling me that I'm not always to blame. Help me begin my inventory by separating true from false guilt.

T. S.

O Lord, I know the way of man is not in himself;
It is not in man who walks to direct his own steps.
—JER. 10:23

In my years of counseling in the area of addictions, more men have lost their recovery over an inner struggle with their will than for any other reason. Almost every day in the hospital, I hear someone say, "If only I could face this issue with my will, I could be in recovery." Men who have struggled with addiction for many years have testified that they have never achieved meaningful sobriety because they've never "turned it over."

Turning it over refers to Step 3 of the Twelve Steps which goes to the very root of man's deepest stronghold, a man's will. Since the beginning of time man has been in a struggle between the flesh and the spirit, his way versus God's way. In the third step a man is told to make a decision to give up control and let God take over. To the addictive personality, asking him to surrender his will is tantamount to asking him to give up his life. In fact, I have seen quite a few men die of their addictions rather than turn over their will to God.

Yes, surrendering your will to God in the area of your addiction is a difficult and life-changing experience. Yet, to fail to do so is to surrender yourself to a cruel and destructive power that will ultimately kill you. Decide to trust God, surrender your will to Him daily, and claim His sovereignty in your life.

Let go and let God.

L. S.

And whatever you do, do it heartily, as to the Lord and not to men, knowing that from the Lord you will receive the reward of the inheritance; for you serve the Lord Christ.　　　—COL. 3:23–24

A great coach once said, "There's only one thing we practice for and that's to win; there's only one thing we play for, and that's to win; there's only one thing we live for, and that's to win; and there's only one thing we do to win—*everything*." Everything his team did was for victory. They practiced and played with precision and intensity. To do any less was to prepare for defeat. Every part of their lives had to be trained on winning, never second best—it wouldn't do.

Another aspect of this story is the players' love for their coach. He had instilled in them this great work ethic and had given them motivation and inspiration to win. As a result they grew to love the coach for his leadership.

Similarly, our lives must be driven to holiness in every aspect. When God speaks of "whatever you do," He means all, our motivation being eternity, our inspiration being the Cross. Out of this is born a growing love for the Savior and willingness to give Him our all.

———————

Lord, I commit all of who I am to You.

B. D.

But now after you have known God, or rather are known by God, how is it that you turn again to the weak and beggarly elements, to which you desire again to be in bondage?   —GAL. 4:9

I used to make regular trips to the quagmire. The quagmire is the place to which my low self-esteem sent me, to mire me down, to make me miserable, to allow me to indulge my favorite character defect—self-pity! I used to tell myself I didn't want to go, but I went anyway, feeling sorrier and sorrier for myself as I went.

The quagmire is in my head. My poor view of myself can send me there in a heartbeat, but more and more I choose not to go. False guilt is sending me to the quagmire.

Inventory after inventory, I find ways to keep from going to the quagmire. I have valuable work to perform for God and can't afford to waste time there. I am better than I thought I was and don't like the quagmire. I have lost my taste for self-pity, and the quagmire doesn't appeal to me as much.

God tells me I need not go to the quagmire. And as I take inventory, I lose my desire to make the trip.

God, please help me to stay out of the quagmire today. Thank You for freeing me through the tenth step.

                                                              T. S.

When my father and my mother forsake me,
Then the LORD will take care of me.
—PS. 27:10

The adult male sexual abuse victim has many deep emotional wounds from the past. The trauma of sexual abuse can be so deep that he passes it down to his children, unconsciously repeating what was done to him.

Males who have been sexually abused experience the world as victims. The male victim often feels that being forced to commit sexual acts meant for adults took part of his childhood from him. He may have a difficult time playing, joking, or allowing others to have fun. He may also have difficulty being assertive and expressing emotions. He may wonder what it is like to live a normal life. The sexually abused male may also be committed to avoiding conflict. His life is likely filled with deep longings for, but fears of trust and intimacy.

Without recovery the sexually abused male goes through life with deep feelings of unworthiness, guilt, and shame.

If you can relate to this life of victimization, you may have been sexually or emotionally abused. It is difficult to reach for help, but if you will trust God, believe that He cares about you, and be willing to tell your story, you can become a survivor.

Admitting that you're a victim is the first step to becoming a survivor.

L. S.

> *Jesus went into the temple and began to drive out*
> *those who bought and sold in the temple, and*
> *overturned the tables of the moneychangers*
> *and the seats of those who sold doves. And He*
> *would not allow anyone to carry wares through*
> *the temple.* —MARK 11:15–16

Anger is a hard emotion for many men to understand and deal with. Here, the Scripture gives us an account of Jesus feeling anger. Jesus was perfect and never sinned, but He did get angry and expressed it righteously.

A sixty-two-year-old pastor named Carl was admitted to the hospital for depression. He stated that at age fifteen he gave his life to God as a full-time Christian minister. As we talked about his life, he shared many situations in which people mistreated him. But, he never could connect the situations to feelings of anger. He told me that as a Christian minister he could not get angry—he saw that as part of the call. As he continued through the recovery process, he became able to find anger a legitimate emotion and to express his anger righteously.

In the recovery process we must often deal with our own anger. Anger is a human emotion that we all feel. It is not bad in itself. It can be expressed in wrong ways or in righteous ways.

God, help me to express my anger in appropriate ways.

B. N.

*Let all bitterness, wrath, anger, clamor, and evil
speaking be put away from you, with all malice.
And be kind to one another.* —EPH. 4:31–32

Don't worry about it! He's a jerk," Art said when I told
him I felt bad about not liking Jim and talking behind
Jim's back. Jim was obnoxious—loud, brash, and forward.

Art's answer didn't reassure me. I still felt bad about
the way I treated Jim, so I called, and Jim was most
gracious, inviting me for lunch at his office. When we
sat down, I told him that I had been cutting him down
behind his back. I told him I was sorry and hoped we
could be friends. Jim's eyes moistened as he answered,
"You know, I've done just about everything I could to
make friends. I even bought a big-screen TV and asked
the guys over to watch the game, but no one came. I've
just about given up. I guess I just don't fit in."

I was shocked—I had pushed away someone who
needed my help. Jim wasn't a bad guy, only different.
He and I agreed to be friends, and we still are. Jim
stayed around the meetings. That was good for him . . .
and even better for me.

---

*God, please help me not to judge people who are different. Remind
me that the meetings are for anyone who wants to get better.*

T. S.

*And my God shall supply all your needs according
to His riches in glory.*
—PHIL. 4:19

Have you ever wondered what life would be like if we only lived by what we needed instead of what we wanted? Life would probably be very different. Most of us would be less tired since we wouldn't have to work so hard. Our marriages would be great. We would spend a lot of time with our wives and kids, and they would think we were the best. We would probably have more time to go fishing and hunting too. And I suspect that we wouldn't want anything. With contentment there is no need to want because our peace is within.

A need is something we have to meet to survive. A want is something we don't need. From a balanced and healthy perspective I am afraid that most of us would have to admit that we have more of what we want than of what we need. To raise a healthy Christian family the scales need to be tipped the other way. The needs of your family should be met to the point that their wants do not supersede their needs. It is important to note here that needs are not only material, but mental, emotional, physical, and spiritual.

Lord, help me to be content with that which You have given me.

L. S.

He who is slow to wrath has great understanding,
But he who is impulsive exalts folly.
—PROV. 14:29

Anticipation." It was a great song from the seventies. It was also used as the sales pitch for a brand of ketchup, the premise being that the ketchup was so good and thick that it was worth the wait.

As long as I can remember, the virtues of patience have been extolled. Be patient because it's safer; it will save more money; it tastes better; you'll appreciate it more. When things are given the time necessary to be thought out and not rushed into, the chance of mistake is decreased.

Patience carries with it self-control, and any man who controls his own temper is wise. This man has learned that patience protects him from exhibiting embarrassing behavior and having to apologize for it. Most importantly, however, as it is joined with prayer, patience mirrors Christ while impulse reflects folly.

Patience is a fruit of the Spirit, and like most fruit, it is at its best when nurtured and grown to maturity.

Lord, help me to be patient in all things and to wait for Your guidance.

B. D.

*Set your mind on things above, not on things on
the earth.*
—COL. 3:2

Resentment is the number one offender. We have to be free of it or it kills us." So says the Big Book of AA. And resentments do creep in if I start becoming concerned with my own dear self. So-and-so doesn't treat me right. Mr. Smith doesn't like me. The kids have no respect. It goes on and on, and I get sicker and angrier and more resentful.

Taking inventory in the tenth step means more than just saying "Sorry." It really requires a change in attitudes. When I fix my gaze on poor little me I lose God's perspective on life, other people, and myself.

Instead, I need to look on heavenly things. How much have I gained in friendships, in good feelings from helping others? How much more than I really need does God give me every single day? I need to change from self-centeredness to gratitude.

That's it! In the tenth step, I will always keep perspective if I have an attitude of gratitude.

God, thank You for reminding me to keep my eyes on You. Please give me the attitude of gratitude today.

T. S.

If anyone will not work, neither shall he eat.
—2 THESS. 3:10

Men often ask if I think that work is a curse. My answer is usually, "God probably intended for us to work even before the Fall, so it's probably not a curse, but it can be a curse if you make it one."

The way we view work says a lot about us. Some men can do the same job for forty years and never complain once. Going to work for them is as natural as eating; they don't even question it. For others, work is a daily burden. They tend to view work as a curse. They feel as though God owes them something, that they are supposed to get a free ride in life.

There would probably be no meaning in life if everything was just given to us. Working enables us to use all the talents and abilities God gave us. Work gives us an opportunity to fulfill part of God's plan for our lives. Work gives us an opportunity to have male friends and to witness to others. Most importantly work enables us to buy a little peace and contentment in life with our home, our land, and our family. Work enables us to have a few weeks of vacation with the family. In most instances, work allows us to spend Sunday with God before returning to work on Monday.

Lord, help me to see work as a blessing rather than a curse.

L. S.

> *Brethren, if a man is overtaken in any trespass, you who are spiritual restore such a one in a spirit of gentleness, considering yourself lest you also be tempted.*
> —GAL. 6:1

When our friends are caught in sin, the Bible encourages us to restore them in a spirit of gentleness.

I knew a man who had become involved with another woman. A friend of his named Chris went to talk with him in a spirit of friendship and support. He approached him about his sin with Christian love and in a spirit of gentleness. The man refused to acknowledge that he had done anything wrong. Chris continued to be a friend by praying for him to turn away from his sin.

Most of us really don't want to get involved when our friends are sinning. Or sometimes we feel justified in letting that friend "have it" for what they have done. The Bible suggests that we get involved and confront the sin. It also tells us to do so in a spirit of gentleness.

Lord, grant me Your gentleness in caring for others.

B. N.

> *But avoid foolish and ignorant disputes, knowing*
> *that they generate strife.* —2 TIM. 2:23

The preamble of Alcoholics Anonymous says, "AA is not allied with any sect, denomination, politics, organization or institution; does not wish to engage in any controversy; neither endorses nor opposes any causes. Our primary purpose is to stay sober and help other alcoholics to achieve sobriety."

The founders of AA knew only too well that foolish disputes generate strife. To help others to get sober, they forsook all other involvements. And that policy has allowed the fellowship to grow and maintain stability for more than fifty years.

How much time do you spend in foolish arguments about the daily trivia of life? I know I do it too much. It would be better to stop for a minute and quietly say, "This doesn't really matter. Why don't we stop arguing and talk about something important?"

God, keep me from silly arguments and discussions today. Help me to spend my time wisely, talking about the important things of life.

T. S.

*There is one who makes himself rich, yet has
  nothing;
And one who makes himself poor, yet has
  great riches.*   —PROV. 13:7

You have heard it said that it's not money but the love of money that is the root of all evil. Possibly the love of social status is the root of most spending. How many men are deeply in debt as a result of trying to maintain a high standard of living? Debt pressure has had a profound impact on American families. Over 70 percent of recent divorces in America involved financial problems.

Most men put themselves and their families under the pressure of financial debt by attempting to provide nice things for their family. Early spending is usually done with the best of a man's intentions; and he is usually praised and rewarded by his family for providing such luxuries. Within months, though, they must be replaced to keep up with what everyone else has. Since most men do not actually have the income to achieve their ideal standard of living, they end up borrowing to reach their goal.

Being in debt makes a man a prisoner of his creditors. Status is not worth the cost of paying the piper.

Lord, please help me become financially debt-free through my hard work so that I may nurture and care for my family.

L. S.

> *But God demonstrates His own love toward us, in*
> *that while we were still sinners, Christ died for us.*
> —ROM. 5:8

Most of us struggle from time to time with feelings of insecurity, doubt, and even worthlessness. We wonder how or if anyone could ever love us. We are so familiar with our own human faults and undesirable traits. This knowledge fuels the fire of low self-esteem. Our mind tells us that because I am what I am, no one would or could ever love me. Most of the time, however, we're not as bad as we seem.

Granted, there are times that we cannot see or feel a lot of "lovability" in ourselves, people may or may not love, encourage, and accept us to the extent that we wish. But there is One who is consistent, forgiving, and never has a lack of love. He is God.

While it is rare that we find a person who would die for another, Christ did just that and more. Christ died for all: the powerless, the ungodly, the sinners, and even His enemies. So the next time you are wondering if anyone loves you and how much, remember that you are the reason Christ demonstrated His divine love.

Thank You, Lord, for Your love for me. It is always sufficient.

B. D.

*Therefore we must give the more earnest heed to
the things we have heard, lest we drift away.*
—HEB. 2:1–3

At about the time we get to the tenth step, many of us begin to relax. We realize we're never going to graduate from Twelve Step groups, so we can afford to go a little slower. That's okay, but we need to be on our guard, lest our relaxation turn to complacency.

If we have taken a thorough moral inventory; admitted our wrongs to ourselves, to God, and to another man; asked God to help us get free of the past; made a list of people we have harmed and made amends to them, we really have come a long way. But the tenth, eleventh, and twelfth steps are the maintenance steps for daily living. If we don't work them vigorously, we risk slipping backward. We must not take our serenity, our recovery, our peace of mind for granted.

So recommit yourself today to sticking with it to the end. Start by taking a tenth-step inventory.

God, help me to guard against complacency. Help me to take an honest spot-check inventory to see how I'm really doing.

T. S.

Since we are surrounded by so great a cloud of witnesses, let us lay aside every weight, and the sin which so easily ensnares us, and let us run with endurance the race that is set before us.
—HEB. 12:1

It is often very difficult for a man to maintain a constant flow of productivity at work. Between a man's own drivenness to perform and his company's expectations, the necessity to produce can become almost unbearable. Companies try to get the most work out of the fewest number of employees and pay the least amount of money to those of whom they expect the most. Today's man is also expected to perform and produce at home, in the community, and at church. Where does a man find the physical strength and mental energy to remain productive?

Practically speaking, the average man probably uses most of his energy trying to produce at his job; he then uses whatever energy is left at home.

The key to facing this dilemma is maintaining balance. God wants us to be wise and prudent stewards of the energy we have. He doesn't want us to spend it all in one place. You are not perfect; you are not a bottomless pit; you are not responsible alone for the company's success; and your first priorities in life are serving God and family.

Balance between job productivity and other responsibilities is so difficult for me, Jesus. Please help me to learn that gentle balance.

L. S.

Unless the LORD builds the house,
They labor in vain who build it.
—PS. 127:1

Men have gotten away from building their families. Many men leave it to their wives or others. God instructed men to be the house builders.

While I was working with Robert and Susie, it became obvious that Robert had never been concerned about heading his household. As we continued to discuss the importance of his role as a husband and a father, he began to take hold of his family and provide leadership. It was amazing to see how his wife and children responded to his leadership.

We have a desperate family breakdown in our society today. Some of this can be attributed to the fathers who abandon their families physically. It can also be attributed to the fathers who abandon their families spiritually or emotionally. Many fathers think they are doing their job by "bringing home the bacon." But there is much more for a father to do than that.

Are you there for your family? Or is the father missing in action in your home?

God, grant me strength and wisdom to be a godly builder of my house today.

B. N.

> *Beloved, since you know these things*
> *beforehand, beware lest you also fall*
> *from your own steadfastness.* —2 PETER 3:17

I took a fourth and fifth step twenty years ago," said Old Steve, the veins in his temples bulging out, "and I've never seen the need to do any of that stuff again!" Of Steve's several nicknames in AA, "Old Steve" is the only one fit to print. He was an irascible old guy who was really okay to those of us who worked hard at getting to know him. He never really had any serenity, even though he had been sober for twenty years.

Many folks share Steve's viewpoint. Why should we do another inventory? Well, let's look at it this way: Any business, regardless of how successful, will not stay in business very long without at least an annual inventory. We simply have to know what we have in stock. We need to know what is of value, what is distressed merchandise, and what is simply old stock of no use at all.

Things change, times change, and we change. We need to keep current with what is going on in our lives and inside our hearts and heads. To do less is to court the consequences of relapse. Anyone care to join me in a tenth step?

God, keep us moving forward in our inventory attempts. Please remind us that if we stop going forward, we are going backward.

T. S.

When a man's ways please the LORD,
He makes even his enemies to be at peace
with him. —PROV. 16:7

You have heard the saying, "First impressions are lasting." Well, for some men every impression is lasting. Some men are obsessively image conscious. They are always trying to look or behave in a certain manner, particularly at work. They constantly predict the reactions of others and attempt to manipulate their internal and external world by maintaining an image.

I used to be image conscious. I always drove the right kind of car, wore the right hairstyle, and had fashion clothes. I constantly rehearsed in my mind what I would or should say to my boss, to assure that he thought positively of me. I did whatever pleased my customers or my supervisors at work. My rewards were acceptance and control.

I am no longer image conscious. Maintaining the image took too much time, money, and energy, so I took on a new way of living. As I changed, I discovered that God loved me for what was in my heart, not for the way I looked or acted. Having found my true significance in God, I was able to be more assertive, say no, and set boundaries. I could make mistakes and still feel okay.

Now when someone asks me what has actually changed in my life, I just say, "I'm no longer trying to win friends and influence people."

Dear God, please help me to learn that the only person I need to please is You.

L. S.

> *Being confident of this very thing, that He who has begun a good work in you will complete it until the day of Jesus Christ.*
> —PHIL. 1:6

I love it when I know something is going to turn out all right, especially when the odds may be against me. It can be anything—a financial decision, a project to be completed, or even a long trip in the car. The one essential ingredient is confidence, which secures your knowledge that you have what it takes to make the right decision and get the job done. Usually we are confident based on past experience, current knowledge, and a lot of faith. Confidence makes the journey more comfortable to travel.

And so it is with our walk in the Lord. Through our faith in Him, we find confidence to move through life's trails. The faith and confidence are based on what Christ did on the Cross and what He is doing today. He lives within us and walks with us daily. As we look to the future we can have confidence that everything will turn out better than okay—it will turn out gloriously.

———————

Lord, may I rest confidently in the knowledge of what You have done for me.

B. D.

*Sought through prayer and meditation to improve
our conscious contact with God as we understood
Him, praying only for knowledge of His will for us
and the power to carry that out.*
—THE TWELVE STEPS OF ALCOHOLICS ANONYMOUS

*Let no one say when he is tempted, "I am tempted
by God"; for God cannot be tempted by evil, nor
does He Himself tempt anyone. But each one is
tempted when he is drawn away by his own
desires and enticed.*   —JAMES 1:13–14

When I tried meditation, all the day's business crossed my mind, crowding out the Spirit of God.

At a Saturday morning prayer meeting we decided to try something different. With the room quiet (no TV or stereo), we all began to pray silently. As other thoughts crossed our minds (mowing the grass, problems at work, money concerns), we put them aside onto the "God pile," all the thoughts that keep us from hearing Him and Him alone.

We focused on emptying our minds of anything that would keep us from hearing the Spirit. After about ten or fifteen minutes, our minds were clear and peaceful, and we felt the presence of God as never before.

The "God pile" works. Simply put every thought that will stand in the way of listening to God on that pile as you pray.

God, it is my intention to be able to meditate on You and You alone. Help me to use the "God pile" to clear my mind as I seek to know You better.

T. S.

But I say to you, love your enemies, bless those who curse you, do good to those who hate you, and pray for those who spitefully use you and persecute you.

—MATT. 5:44

One of the most uncomfortable situations for a man to find himself in is working for a "toxic boss." A toxic boss is virtually impossible to please, no matter what or how much one does. He is unpredictable, moody, driven, irritable, forward, critical, and rarely encouraging. Everyone outwardly respects and obeys him, but inwardly hates and resists. He must always be in control. A man never knows if the toxic boss is truly for him or against him because so many double messages are given off.

How can a man protect himself against toxicity? Assuming that he must stay in the situation to make a living, he will need to realize that the root of his boss's toxicity is a deep insecurity and inferiority complex. This type of boss overcompensates by maintaining such an ego and by overcontrolling others. Do not internalize the toxic behavior by taking it personally. To maintain your integrity and self-respect, have boundaries, and be assertive, remembering what Jesus said about servanthood. Remember that Jesus is your main boss. He is the one you and even your boss ultimately have to answer to.

Heavenly Father, help me to have a genuine caring spirit for those in leadership at my job.

L. S.

*God created man in His own image; in the image
of God He created him; male and female He
created them.* —GEN. 1:27

The trend in the world today is not to distinguish between the sexes. We see "unisex" clothes and hair-
styles. However, God did create man and woman differently. There are certain distinctions that should not
be ignored.

Ken came to counseling because he was struggling
with his sexual identity. His father divorced his mother
when Ken was eight months old, so he never had a
strong male role model. Ken was confused about masculinity. He thought being male meant being macho,
being interested in sports, or being like John Wayne.

In our talks we looked at masculinity as being a
strong initiator. The Bible emphasizes male leadership.
Masculinity has less to do with the way we dress and
wear clothes, etc. True masculinity is being open to
God's leadership and having a positive impact on our
world. It involves taking hold of our inadequacies, accepting those we cannot change, and changing the
ones we can. Real men find an inner strength in their
relationship with God.

*Lord, thanks for giving me a special distinctiveness. Help me to enjoy
being a man.*

B. N.

> *Brethren, I commend you to God and to the word*
> *of His grace, which is able to build you up and*
> *give you an inheritance among all those who are*
> *sanctified.*
> —ACTS 20:32

Mike's wife was determined to divorce him. He had done some things wrong, but he wanted to stay married and work it out. His wife, Sue, would have none of it. She wanted a divorce.

Maybe you, too, have been forced to accept the unthinkable. How does a man get through a time like that?

Mike and I talked about "moving into the eleventh step." Simply put, it means living every moment of every day just asking to know God's will for us and to have the strength to do it.

Mike lost his job, his enthusiasm, and most of his money. But he stayed sober. Each day, looking for work, he asked God for the strength to struggle through job hunting. After he got a job, he asked for the strength to do it.

Today Mike is okay. He is still divorced, not remarried, still working. And every day he asks God for knowledge of His will and strength to carry it out.

God, help us to keep our prayers simple when we go through tough times.

T. S.

Seek first the kingdom of God and His righteousness, and all these things shall be added to you.
—MATT. 6:33

When Brad came for counseling, he shared with me that his wife had run off and left him. She had left behind only a single note on the refrigerator door: "Dear Brad, you have been in love with your job for ten years, and now you can marry her for good." Brad's marriage ended as a result of workaholism. In the beginning of the marriage Brad was home all of the time and had a fiery romantic relationship with his wife. Over time, however, he spent less time at home and more time at his job. When his wife questioned him about spending so much time at work, he got defensive saying, "A man has to work to provide for his family. Anyway, things will slow down soon." However, things at work never slowed down for Brad.

Brad never planned to be a workaholic. He was slowly drawn into the vicious cycle of taking a large degree of his self-worth and value from work. As he spent more time at work, he obviously worked less at being a father and husband. Communication and parenting problems developed at home, and the worse things got, the more he worked.

Brad's wife unfortunately never returned to the marriage, but he sought to recover from workaholism and he realized that his self-respect was based on being, rather than doing.

Jesus, please help me to learn that my self-worth should be based on heavenly things, not things of this world, which will pass away.

L. S.

> *. . . whom I shall see for myself,*
> *And my eyes shall behold, and not another.*
> *How my heart yearns within me!*
> —JOB 19:27

In 1968, as the Vietnam war was at its peak, my father went off to that faraway land to serve his country. The good-bye was painful and the adjustment difficult, but there was nothing to do but let go. I loved my father very much, and I missed being with him. Months went by, and finally we got word that he was coming home. Joy filled my heart as I thought of his return. I would see him again! When the day came, my body ached from excitement. Finally, there he was. I could hardly believe it, and I wouldn't have had I not seen it with my own eyes. To see his eyes looking at me again as my father, oh, how I yearned for that.

As great a feeling as this was for me, it cannot compare with seeing the heavenly Father face to face. This is every believer's desire. The day my father got off that plane, he was not alone, but he was all I could see. When we are in heaven, there will be nothing else greater to look forward to than to see God, for there is none greater.

Father, keep my eyes fixed on You until I see You face to face.

B. D.

If you abide in My word, you are My disciples indeed. And you shall know the truth, and the truth shall make you free. —JOHN 8:31–32

In my first three years around AA, I struggled with knowing the truth. I had lied so consistently that I needed to start from the ground up regarding truth. The truth about God's will for me was particularly troublesome. What if God's will was not what I wanted? What if I was mistaken about His will?

During most of my fourth year, I complained about my life, got angry at God, and wore out most of my friends. I also learned how to pray. I told the Lord all about my life, myself, and other people that I didn't like. I let Him know just how angry I was about my situation. But I always prayed, in the spirit of the eleventh step, "Nevertheless, in this and all things, Thy will, not my will, be done."

How did it all turn out? Well, things still don't go my way, and my life is still very much the same, but that's okay. You see, I know the truth today, and the truth has set me free . . . to be me.

God, thank You for setting me free today.

T. S.

We also glory in tribulations, knowing that
tribulation produces perseverance; and
perseverance, character; and character, hope.
—ROM. 5:3–4

Has the romance gone out of your job? Do you feel unappreciated and taken advantage of? Do you believe that the company has forgotten about you, or that you are never going to move up with the company? If you answer yes to any of these questions, then you are probably suffering from burnout, job dissatisfaction along with an absence of energy and motivation to remain functional in the job.

One of the first signs of burnout is depression or apathy at work, then fatigue and lack of energy. A man's production level may decrease, and he may begin to find reasons to miss work. A major symptom is not wanting to go to work.

Male victims of job burnout usually have similar work habits and personalities. They are driven, trying to do more than they can handle and finding it hard to say no. These men also usually neglect family time, recreation, leisure, and spiritual development.

To avoid burnout at your job you must maintain a balanced life and set limits on your hours at work. Sometimes our expectations for ourselves can be higher than God's are for us.

Lord, help me to discover the balance that I need in my life.

L. S.

You will show me the path of life;
In Your presence is fullness of joy;
At Your right hand are pleasures
*   forevermore.*   —PS. 16:11

Men are yearning for leadership. They want someone to give them direction. Most men are searching for a missing father figure. The men's movement is addressing this need for many men. Seminars and conferences are being held all over the country to help men to grieve the absence of a father who gave them unconditional love and acceptance.

As I watch the nation's response to General Norman Schwartzkopf, I could see that people are drawn to strong male leaders. He was a central figure in the war with Iraq. We felt secure knowing our men were in his hands. He helped to give us a sense that things were going to work out.

God wants to provide us with a path to life. We can feel safe in His plans. The path He provides is found by trust in Jesus Christ. Have you trusted Jesus for eternal life? God is the true answer to your father-hunger.

God, help me to look to You today to find a path to live by.

                                                    B. N.

> *He shall be like a tree*
> *Planted by the rivers of water,*
> *That brings forth its fruit in its season,*
> *Whose leaf also shall not wither;*
> *And whatever he does shall prosper.*
> —PS. 1:3

Do you have one friend who models Christ for you? I do. His name is Jim. If I need something, a kind word, encouragement, help with money, Jim is there.

Jim is fruitful. He started from the ground up and now has a large business that allows him to hire men who need a second chance. You see, Jim had a second chance once, and now he delights in helping others.

Jim is consistent. Even when I don't see him for months, our friendship is firm, assured, and constant.

Jim is also prosperous. His business grows each year, allowing Jim to give more away. His generosity has saved many people financially.

Jim succeeds because he is planted by the river of God's truth. He works at the eleventh step each day, seeking to know God's will. He is constantly nourished by the truth of God's Word. I think I'll tell Jim today how much I appreciate him.

God, I pray that all men might have a Jim in their life. Please lead me to such a man if I don't know one now.

T. S.

Do not overwork to be rich;
Because of your own understanding,
cease!
—PROV. 23:4

Many psychologists support the concept of positive stress, stress that motivates and stimulates a man to interact with his world in a positive way. At work a man may be motivated to meet a sales quota in order to avoid stress that he would encounter as a result of not meeting the quota. However, as this man is driven to meet more and more quotas in the future, he also maintains a continual exposure to what I call negative stress. Although positive stress creates a positive outcome for the employer, it creates a negative physical and psychological outcome for the employee.

Negative stress wears on a man over time, draining him of energy, willpower, and physical strength. It can lead to depression and to emotional and physical collapse.

To deal with the exposure to negative stress, some men have made drastic changes in their lives. Many have cut back on their daily work hours and even the number of days they work each week. Other men have taken up hobbies, leisure activities, and exercise programs to offset the stress.

Finally, in dealing with negative stress it is a good idea to look at the life of Jesus. He was subjected to profound stress, yet He continued to model a healthy and balanced life.

Remember that there are limits to how much stress any man can bear.

L. S.

> *I know that whatever God does,*
> *It shall be forever.*
> —ECCL. 3:14

The giant redwoods of our national parks are a testimony to strength and longevity. Spiraling skyward, reaching heavenly heights, these trees are admired for their beauty and their history. Men consider these trees masterpieces and treasures of nature. We could never manufacture something comparable. As we come to appreciate them even more, we are confident that they will stand forever.

Man's structures and machines are as he is—temporary. Buildings fall every day and machinery gives out. Money is invested daily to improve, to study, and to attempt to construct "eternal" structures. Meanwhile the trees grow freely, seedlings sprouting up by God's design, God's nurture, and God's hand. This tree will transcend generations, not from man's toil, but instead from an eternal God.

The God of eternity has touched our lives as well. As we grow, we can be assured that as a result we will "last forever." We can do nothing to separate us from the love of God. Truly, what God does is forever.

Father God, You are sovereign, and there is nothing that is present that was not touched by You.

B. D.

*Assuredly, I say to you, whoever does not receive
the kingdom of God as a little child will by no
means enter it.* —MARK 10:15

One of my earliest memories is of sitting in the dining room of our old house as my mother played an old Sunday school song about God "looking down in love" on our decrepit piano. One day, I scrunched down underneath the narrow keyboard, tucked my knees under my chin, and said, "Mama, can He see me hiding way under here?"

"Yes, He sees you there. . . . He sees you no matter where you go."

That bothered me. I wanted some right to privacy, some time to myself. I should be able to do and to think whatever I wanted without being watched. I wanted God when I needed Him, but not at other times.

Through Twelve Step meetings I have learned to draw great pleasure and security from the knowledge that no matter where I go, God sees me. He is an all-knowing, all-seeing, and caring Father, "looking down in love."

God, thank You for Your faithful watch-care over me, even when I don't want it. I pray I will grow in love and seek You every moment of the day.

T. S.

> *The sleep of a laboring man is sweet,*
> *Whether he eats little or much;*
> *But the abundance of the rich will not*
> *permit him to sleep.*
>
> —ECCL. 5:12

When was the last time you can remember that you weren't tired? Maybe it was when you were a little boy and were full of energy. Or perhaps it was during your last real vacation. Perhaps it has been so long that you cannot remember.

Most men run their lives in the red in terms of available physical and psychic energy. Physical energy enables the body to keep running; psychic energy enables the mind to stay in business. Most of us men tend to think that we somehow maintain an endless reserve of energy. In truth, though, once we have spent energy in one area of our life, it is not available to be spend in another area.

Every time we walk, talk, move, think, listen, or feel, it costs us a certain amount of energy. If we spend 75 percent of our energy at work, we in turn have little energy to spend at home with the family or on other important areas of our lives.

Manage your energy as a valuable resource, remembering that it should first go to God and your family.

Lord, help me to be a wise steward of the energy which You give me daily.

L. S.

> *. . . speaking the truth in love, may grow up in all things into Him who is the head—Christ.*
>
> —EPH. 4:15

Many men do not know how to express or show love. It is especially hard for men to show love when confronting another person. It is also hard for men to be honest with others. Honesty requires that you are committed to the other person's best, no matter what.

I remember going to a friend to talk with him about some problems I was seeing in his life. I became aware afterward that I had not gone in a spirit of love. The words I spoke were true, but were not spoken in love. One of the reasons the person did not respond to me was that he did not sense a spirit of love.

Honesty and love are important to healthy relationships. But it does take more than a willingness to face tough issues in others. It sometimes requires having to look at many of our own issues.

May I be honest with others in an attitude and spirit of love today.

B. N.

But seek the kingdom of God, and all these things shall be added to you. —LUKE 12:27–34

What is God's will for you? How can you know it? These questions filled my mind when I first read the eleventh step. Of course, I was looking for God's will with the eyes of an egotist. I imagined myself as a charismatic evangelist, saving, with God's help of course, thousands of seeking sinners. Or perhaps I would be a missionary pilot, flying supplies and crates full of Bibles into dangerous jungle clearings. Perhaps God would use me to reach many who suffered from addiction and alcoholism. And so on . . . and on.

We can know God's will one moment at a time. For example, when the alarm goes off in the morning, unless I am very sick, it is God's will for me to go to work. At dinnertime, it is God's will that I prepare and eat my dinner. When someone I know is struggling, it is God's will for me to help. God's will, instead of being some herculean deed I do while thousands of adoring people look on, is accomplished in my life when I pay attention to the ordinary, letting God lead as He will.

God, help me to see what Your will is for me in my daily life, in the regular and ordinary things I do.

T. S.

*Those who desire to be rich fall into temptation
and a snare, and into many foolish and harmful
lusts which drown men in destruction and
perdition.*   —1 TIM. 6:9

It is amazing to me what high prices some men are willing to pay to carry the checkered flag just once in their career. For some men job success is almost their entire life.

Men who are career and success driven actually believe that by achieving their career goal, they will also find the meaning of their lives. They also believe that a certain degree of success will bring security and happiness to the family. These beliefs could not be further from the truth. First, Jesus said that true happiness cannot be found in material things alone, but in a spiritual relationship with God. Second, I hear often from my patients, "My daddy was always at work, so I didn't feel as important."

When we find ourselves getting into the practice of workaholism and achievement-based happiness, our wives and children pay for most of it. Our wives pay by spending endless hours alone and without ever experiencing the true love that a husband can give. Our children miss out on a nurturing friendship with a dad.

Is your family paying for your career success? Can you can continue to let them?

Be sure that you can pay the interest on your success when the payment comes due.

L. S.

> *Let us come before His presence with thanksgiving;*
> *Let us shout joyfully to Him with psalms.*
>
> —PS. 95:2

Mad? You think I'm mad? I'm livid! Not a 'thank you,' a 'good job,' or even a 'not bad.' Nothing. I deserve better!"

How many times have you heard this chorus or even felt it yourself?

It's always nice to be appreciated, to have a sense that our work and who we are are noticed. It seems, though, the only time we are noticed is when something goes wrong. Imagine being the Creator of the universe, the giver of life, and the loving, sovereign God that gave His only Son for mankind. Continue to consider what it must feel like to have done all of this and rarely be given a word of thanks, be spoken to only when your beloveds need something or question why.

Although we cannot suppose to feel as God does, we do know that we deserve nothing but have been given everything by a loving, unconditionally accepting Father, God.

God is many things to us all. He alone is worthy of our praise. Are you praising Him daily?

Heavenly Father, You alone are sovereign; You alone are worthy of psalms.

B. D.

Father, if it is Your will, remove this cup from Me;
nevertheless not My will, but Yours, be done.
—LUKE 22:42

As a fallen man, I have spent much time seeking mercy, justice, grace, and something we call fairness. When childhood games went against me, I hollered at the top of my lungs, "Unfair!" The ultimate in unfair acts was the Lord Jesus' crucifixion for our sins. Alone in the night, His closest friends unable even to stay awake for Him, He faced the events to follow. He was falsely accused, beaten senseless, mocked, spit upon, driven like an animal, betrayed by His friends, nailed to a cross, and left to die. And He was not guilty.

Knowing all this in advance, Jesus prayed as we should in the eleventh step, "Not My will, but Yours." Saved by His act of love for me, can I do less than echo His words by seeking to know and do His will today?

Father, thanks for sending Your son Jesus to die for me. Let me know Your will for me, and strengthen me to carry it out.

T. S.

It is God who works in you both to will and to do for His good pleasure.
—PHIL. 2:13

Every man makes hundreds of thousands of decisions in his life. Many of these decisions are minor and take little or no thought or effort. Then there are major decisions that do have great power and influence over a man's life—decisions to get married, what career to choose, and whether to be a Christian. Other decisions a man makes affect the lives of those around him—like how he spends the family money, whether he has an affair, or how he spends his time.

Decision-making is one of the most important and difficult tasks for a man. Making decisions is difficult because there are many unknowns, and many variables, and other people to consider.

Basically man has to face decisions pertaining to morals, values, and significant others, and God's will. Moral decisions are black or white. A man is either committed to being obedient to God and to his conscience or he isn't. Value decisions are primarily based on what is most important to a man. If a man's priorities are right, then his decisions will tend to follow. Decisions that affect significant others are based on what is best for them in the long run. Finally, God's will ought to shape all the decisions a man makes.

The solitary choices of a man can leave him alone in the end.

L. S.

Rejoice with those who rejoice, and weep with those who weep. —ROM. 12:15

As men we probably have few if any friends that we can weep with. Having friends with whom you can share both the good times and the bad times is essential.

When I recently spent time with a friend, he shared with me some struggles that he was having with his daughter. She was pulling away from the family and running with the wrong crowd. He was really scared that something serious might happen to her. His wife had been struggling with depression as a result of the daughter's behavior. As we talked and as he poured out the pain that was in his heart, we wept together. It was a growing experience for us both. Those kind of friends help us live a balanced life.

Can you weep alone? Can you weep with a friend?

Lord, give me friends who are not afraid to weep or rejoice with me.

B. N.

If anyone is a hearer of the word and not a doer, he is like a man observing his natural face in a mirror; for he observes himself, goes away, and immediately forgets what kind of man he was.
—JAMES 1:22–27

What would I like to change about myself today? Absolutely nothing! God made me who I am. I'm forty-five. I'm losing my hair, wear dentures, and wear a hearing aid. I don't see well with or without my glasses. I'm ten pounds overweight or recently have been or very soon will be again. I have an average intellect and an intense disposition . . . and God loves me very much. He always has! And He always will!

Sometimes when I wake up, I'm bothered by the man in the mirror: crow's feet, gray hair, a little bit slower, a little pudgy. But then I am reminded that the Lord has work for that man today. Regardless of my reservations, I place what I am and have at the Lord's disposal on a daily basis. What happens? I begin to forget about my troubles and to see how truly great the Lord is.

_____

Lord, thank You for loving the man in the mirror. Thanks for letting me see him this morning as You see him.

T. S.

I have learned in whatever state I am, to be content.
—PHIL. 4:11

The best way to describe some of the men I've met is to say that they were jacks of all trades and masters of none. How many men do you know who are this way? They cannot seem to find their work niche; they hop from one career or from one position to another.

Although most of us probably do not fit this description entirely, we may be able to remember a time when we did. I have worked numerous odd jobs. Some of them got me through school, and I worked the other jobs because I thought that was all I could do. I have made three major career moves since high school. In my present career I have gone through numerous specialties and have held numerous clinical positions. Recently, the Lord has shown me that I need to find a course and learn to stay with it until He directs me otherwise.

Many of us cannot be content to just stay on one course long enough to master it. We may see what someone else is doing and think it would be fulfilling to do the same. Others of us have deep fears of success or failure and sabotage ourselves to avoid facing the fear.

God is not the author of fear or confusion, and double-mindedness is not the road to stability. Do what you were created to do; let others do the same; and whatever you do, do it well.

Be slow to give up what you have.

L. S.

But the Lord is faithful, who will establish you and guard you from the evil one. —2 THESS. 3:3

As we bought our first house we were told there would be little things to be done. We painted and carpeted and generally spruced it up. One thing, though, that my wife was more concerned about was placing new deadbolt locks on the doors. It's sad to think of all the fears that we live with day to day. I travel quite a bit and must know that my wife and son are secure and safe. By putting the locks on the doors, I was letting my family know that I loved them and would protect them. Protection is essential as well as keeping intruders away. This is what the locks do.

Jesus Christ is our security. As we ask Him into our hearts, He stands guard at the door protecting us from evil. Life brings us all kinds of trials, temptations, and adversity. It is Christ who offers security from the adversary, keeping evil away.

As you may be going through a difficult time of trial or temptation, you can know that you are secure in Christ and that He will protect you.

Lord, You are my safety and refuge in a troubled time.

B. D.

*Having had a spiritual awakening as a result of
these steps, we tried to carry this message to
alcoholics, and to practice these principles in
all our affairs.*
—THE TWELVE STEPS OF ALCOHOLICS ANONYMOUS

*My food is to do the will of Him who sent Me, and
to finish His work.*   —JOHN 4:34

Those who practice the Twelve Steps of AA do what
they call "Twelve-Step work." They try to practice the
principles in all the steps and to carry the message of
recovery and wholeness to other sufferers.

One night, I left a meeting depressed. I had been too
caught up in myself to get something to help me at the
meeting. I cried out in desperation, "God, please give
me something to do so I can make it through the
night."

When I arrived home, a voice called out of the night
to me, and Cliff walked out of the shadows carrying a
suitcase. He was about twenty-five and had a sad history of dysfunctional family and mental illness. "You
said if I ever needed a place to go, I should come here,"
he said. "Well, here I am."

That night I listened to another frightful tale of argument and abuse at his house. I settled him in and went
to bed. As I closed my eyes, I said, "Thank You, Jesus,
for sending me someone to help."

---

*God, grant me the willingness to help a fellow sufferer. Thank You for
the fact that they help me to know You even more than I help them.*
                                                              T. S.

> *Pursue peace with all men, and holiness, without which no one will see the Lord.* —HEB. 12:14

Steve sat in my office, furious that his employer of eight years had fired him. According to Steve, he was a hard worker, rarely missed a day of work, and made the company a lot of money. This is not the entire story though. Steve was a victim of his own drivenness to succeed. He had been a bridge burner for eight years. Now, when he needed the bridges, they were not there for him to cross. Steve was actually fired because he made a major error and lost one of the company's major accounts. Steve might have saved his job, but the people who were directly involved were the same ones he had walked over earlier. Had he not done so, they might have been supportive.

One saying I am constantly reminded of in my own business is, "Don't burn bridges behind you because you never know when you'll have to cross them again." Statements like "you reap what you sow" and "what goes around comes around" become real to a man when he feels a bridge falling beneath his feet. As Christian men we need to deal with people in the right spirit on a daily basis. You never know when you will need them to have the right spirit in turn one day.

Do unto others as you would like them to do unto you one day.

L. S.

Behold, I will send you Elijah the prophet
Before the coming of the great and dreadful
   day of the LORD.
And he will turn
The hearts of the fathers to the children.
And the hearts of the children to their
   fathers.
Lest I come and strike the earth with a curse.
                              —MAL. 4:5–6

Many men are recognizing the importance the role of the father in a child's life. Part of this is a result of men becoming more aware of their own father-hunger.

While attending a fathering conference, I had the opportunity to meet Dave Simmons who started the ministry, "Dad, the Family Shepherd." He asked me if I knew what the last two verses in the Old Testament were. I had to admit I did not. As he shared them with me, I was amazed. God was talking about restoring the hearts of the fathers to their children and the hearts of the children to their fathers. God sees the importance of the role of the father.

Part of recovery for fathers is restoring their hearts to their children. The role of fathers has a great deal of influence on the world. Don't overlook this important role.

Father, help me be the dad to my children. Turn my heart toward my home.

                                                  B. N.

*Therefore we are ambassadors for Christ, as
though God were pleading through us: we implore
you on Christ's behalf, be reconciled to God.*
                                —2 COR. 5:20

The twelfth step is a real opportunity for Christian
men to share their faith in Christ with others. But just
as the twelve traditions of AA recommend attraction
rather than promotion, we must be sure to share by
example and not simply in words.

Glen was the first person to accept Christ by my witness. It took three and a half years. When I first met
Glen, he thought he was agnostic, which is not uncommon for alcoholics in early recovery. As I sponsored
him into AA, we talked often about God, never about
Christ.

Over the months and years, Glen observed my life,
imperfect but centered on God and in Christ. He asked
questions about what I believe. He began to attend
church with me on Sundays. Slowly, asking, seeking,
Glen came to understand the gospel and to accept
Christ on Christmas 1982. God's Spirit will do the work
if we live for Christ as best we can.

*God, thank You for allowing me the privilege to witness for You. Help
me to be sensitive to fellow sufferers and to live for You one day
at a time.*

                                                        T. S.

You shall not steal.
—EX. 20:15

You would probably be extremely offended if anyone ever called you a thief. You would likely say, "Well, I've never taken anything from anyone." If we looked at ourselves closely enough, we could all admit to occasions when we took from an employer—a pen, a tool, a note pad, or photocopies.

As I reflect on my own life I can recall several times when I stole from employers. While in college I worked at several fast food restaurants as a cook. I sometimes ate food I didn't pay for. I have also taken pens from work and put the photocopier to personal use.

We justify committing minor thefts in the workplace by minimizing our actions. We also rationalize our behavior, telling ourselves that everyone else does it or that it's just a perk that comes with the job. The biggest lie that some men tell themselves is, "The company owes me—I'm just collecting what's mine." The most likely explanation is that we just unconsciously don't feel that we should have to pay for things, so we take opportunities to get things for free.

The next time you're at work and choose to take something, ask yourself if God would be pleased and if you would feel good if others knew about it. If your answer is no, you're probably about to do something you shouldn't.

If you didn't pay for it, then don't take it.

L. S.

*But put on the Lord Jesus Christ, and make no
provision for the flesh, to fulfill its lusts.*
—ROM. 13:14

I would like to share a great analogy with you, one
that exemplifies the power that Christ gives to us.

Picture, if you will, a glove lying on a table. As it
remains there it is lifeless, flat, and is of little benefit.
Place your hand inside the glove, however, and a great
transformation takes place. As your hand fills the
glove, stretching into every space, the glove comes
alive. Lifeless before, it now takes on the character and
strength of the hand, moving as the hand moves, void
without it.

Have you considered life without Christ? Without
Christ, we too are lifeless, flat, and of little benefit. As
Christ enters our lives, we are given a new life full of
vitality. We are injected with joy and moved from flat
to full. And finally we are of immense value and benefit now and for eternity. Allowing Christ into your life is
the key. As you do, you experience the strength and
character of the Lord Jesus.

Putting on Christ is essentially the same thing as putting Him *in* us. Either way, we have life because of
Him.

Lord Jesus, help me to find joy daily in my life with You.

B. D.

*Bear one another's burdens, and so fulfill the law
of Christ.*   —GAL. 6:2

I just spoke to Hank on the phone. I'm moving to a new apartment next week and asked to borrow his truck. I knew he would say yes. He always does. I've been burned out lately, and Hank has been concerned about me. He told me so. Recently, I've taken some steps to lighten my work load, and Hank counseled me throughout that process.

Hank is my trusted friend. He helps me by listening to me and asking me questions. He makes suggestions, always aware that I may make a different choice. But I need his viewpoint.

Obviously, such a relationship works two ways. I give Hank my viewpoint on his situation. I listen to him and tell him of my concerns for him. We communicate, share, bear one another's burdens.

I can't say that I will need Hank or have him around for the rest of my life. Only God knows that. But I will always need someone, like Hank, to help me bear my burdens.

————————

God, thanks for providing someone to help carry the load. I pray I may help someone carry his burden today.

T. S.

> *Lying lips are an abomination to the LORD,*
> *But those who deal truthfully are His delight.*
> —PROV. 12:22

How far would you go to make a dollar if you really needed it and if you were fairly sure you could make it? Some men would do anything to make a dollar.

Almost every profession offers opportunities for dishonesty. Sales, advertising, and investment are among the most vulnerable. In this age of strong business competition, companies encourage their employees to do whatever they have to do to close the deal. Men are seduced into misleading their customers, making false claims, and outright lying to close a deal. A salesman once bragged to me that he could convince anyone that he needed his product. An insurance broker managed to convince his patrons that there was no need to read the fine print on their insurance contracts. It's just as easy to be dishonest by not giving certain information as it is to be dishonest by giving false information.

In today's work force a man can find it difficult not to get caught up into dishonest business practices. All the money and success seem to come to those who are dishonest and honesty doesn't get us anywhere. When you sense this, remember God's promise of provision for you and your family.

Put your sufficiency in God's hands rather than in the grip of a lying tongue.

L. S.

I will instruct you and teach you in the way
* you should go;*
I will guide you with My eye. —PS. 32:8

Growing up was and is hard, especially today. No matter what generation you came from, you have your own stories to tell. For all of us there was the uncertainty and fear of various decisions and situations. We didn't have answers, but boy, did we have questions. There were, however, people we could go to for help and advice. Family, friends, teachers, or pastors, there was hopefully someone available.

As we grew older the questions became more complex, and at times there was no clear answer.

Now we are men with man-sized questions and man-sized concerns. Our problems can be debilitating. Greater still is the tragedy of "going it alone." God the Father has offered Himself as our counselor. When we will not or cannot speak with others, we can rest assured that He is there to guide and direct us. We also find comfort in His instruction.

As you seek answers in life, what greater advisor do you have than the almighty, all-knowing God? Go to Him, He *will* guide you.

Lord, I will seek Your wisdom and counsel as I move forward in life.
B. D.

> *He has delivered us from the power of darkness
> and translated us into the kingdom of the Son of
> His love.*
> —COL. 1:13

What is a spiritual awakening? According to *Alcoholics Anonymous* (the Big Book), it is a "personality change sufficient to bring about recovery." The Big Book goes on to say that the first printing of the book gave "the impression that these personality changes, or religious experiences, must be in the nature of sudden and spectacular upheavals. Happily for everyone, this conclusion is erroneous."

The spiritual experiences or awakenings most common today among workers of the Twelve Steps is what "the psychologist William James called the 'educational variety' because they develop slowly over a period of time." As we work the steps in order, we begin to develop a hopefulness. We slowly move into a position of service to God and our fellowman.

Thank You, God, for new perspectives on You, on my fellowman, and on myself. Help me to be of service today.

T. S.

We urge you, brethren, to recognize those who labor among you, and are over you in the Lord and admonish you, and to esteem them very highly in love for their work's sake. Be at peace among yourselves.   —1 THESS. 5:12–13

A position of leadership at work is both a privilege and a tremendous responsibility. Being a leader means that you are accountable to those who are under you. Jesus, the master leader, said that He came to serve. In many ways this seems irrational since you would expect us to serve Him. Jesus' example brings us to the point of seriously examining our leadership on the job.

If you had to literally answer to God at the end of your shift as a supervisor, what do you think He would say about the way you deal with those under you? Would He be well pleased? Or would He be disappointed?

A good leader sees himself as a servant to those who are under him. He sees others as equals as much as it is possible to do so in the work place. After all, in God's eyes all of us are equal. A good leader is more a listener than a talker, an encourager and a motivator than a criticizer. He brings out the best in others and enables them to be all they can be.

If you serve those under you, they will want to act like your masters.

L. S.

I also labor, striving according to His working
which works in me mightily. —COL. 1:27–29

What does carrying the message of the Twelve Steps mean? To me it means helping other alcoholics to stop drinking by introducing them to AA. It means being available when someone reaches out for help. It means holding up my end of relationships with recovering friends as we "trudge the road of happy destiny" together. Finally, it means keeping my own sobriety and serenity by giving it away.

Just as we must have certain attitudes to carry the message, there are certain things we must not do. We have an old saying, "You can carry the message, but you must not carry the sufferer." We cannot support another sick person by making life easy for him. Of course we feed the hungry, clothe the naked, and give shelter. But beyond those things, we must not enable a fellow sufferer by making life too easy. We need to practice tough love along with caring love if we are to be really effective in helping others.

God, thank You for the opportunity for service that You have provided in the Twelve Steps. Give me discernment when I reach out to others.

T. S.

Do not overwork to be rich;
Because of your own
understanding, cease!
—PROV. 23:4

Men find much of their reinforcement and praise from how well they perform at work. Many men even find their self-worth wrapped up in their professions and jobs. This is why it is not unusual to find many male workaholics.

Leon had built a large company and had made millions of dollars. He had almost every material need and want taken care of. He had established himself as the leader in his industry. Yet, he realized he was not happy. His wife and children had suffered a lot of neglect as he worked his way to the top. Only once he "had it all" did he realize that he had gained something that could never completely satisfy.

By the time Leon read this verse, he had recognized it in his own life. The world tells us to make the most money we can, even if that means working twelve to sixteen hours a day or more and not taking time out to rest. God tells us that we need to have our priorities straight. Leon's investments in his health, wife, and family were bankrupt. He had a great deal of changing to do later in life.

Lord, give me wisdom to establish appropriate boundaries on my time at work.

B. N.

> *. . . that you would have a walk worthy of God*
> *who calls you into His own kingdom and glory.*
> —1 THESS. 2:10–12

I have a walk worthy of God when I practice the third part of the twelfth step. We try to "practice these principles" in our daily lives.

First, we need to realize our powerlessness over people, places, and things and that we cannot, without God's help, manage our lives. We need to let God have a daily say in how we run our lives. We should take a searching, fearless inventory of ourselves from time to time. We should have someone to talk with when we are bothered. We need to admit our failures and struggles to God, another person, and ourselves. We should humbly petition God for help with our character flaws. We need to keep our relationships in good order. We need to work at an ever-improving relationship with God by talking and listening to Him. Finally, we need to reach out to others, sharing what God has done in our lives through the Twelve Steps.

None of us will get close to perfect performance with this list of principles, but we can use it as a guideline to daily living.

God, please help me to do my best as I try to practice these principles. Give me patience to enjoy progress without seeking perfection.

T. S.

I have learned in whatever state I am, to be content.
—PHIL. 4:11

Most men probably are never actually satisfied with their work history. Men who view work as a curse from God work with an underlying attitude of frustration and self-pity. Some men accept work as a fact of life and faithfully punch the clock without fail until they retire. These men usually work the same job and the same hours for twenty to thirty years. Then there are men who go from job to job and position to position, never discovering job contentment.

It has been said that only millionaires get to do what they really want to do in life. Other men work at the job of second or third choice, only wishing that they could have the money or freedom to fulfill their life's dream. Some men turn out to be workaholics who sacrificed their lives, physical health, and in some cases their families, just to obtain a handful of promotions and a few more coins in their treasure chest.

In seeking job contentment, a man must identify his needs, examine his vocational goals, and redefine his work role and work philosophy. A man's job must meet his need for a sense of achievement and being a part of something. His vocational goals ought to be realistic, in line with his natural abilities, and parallel to God's will and purpose. A Christian man is to have the heart of a servant to those above and below him.

I want to have contentment and peace about my lot in life, Jesus. Please teach me Your way through the Holy Spirit.

L. S.

*For we are His workmanship, created in Christ
Jesus for good works, which God prepared
beforehand that we should walk in them.*
—EPH. 2:10

Surely the twelfth step, taken whole, is a tall order for
any of us. But the point is for us to make progress, not
gain perfection. In fact, the only part of the steps that
we can work perfectly is the first part of Step 1: "We
admitted we were powerless. . . ." When we apply that
powerlessness to the other steps, we do our best.

No, Step 12 is much too demanding for us to do perfectly. We need God's help just to begin to try.

*God, thank You for the Twelve Steps. Please help me as I seek to
understand and to do the twelfth step to the best of my ability.*

T. S.

Do not be deceived: "Evil company corrupts
good habits."
                                                    —1 COR. 15:33

Some men start off in a positive direction, but are slowly led astray. Men long for peer acceptance and friendships with other males. Because of their own insecurities, sometimes they compromise their values to get this acceptance.

A woman named Rhoda came to see me. She described her marriage as starting out strong. She had felt good about their relationship. However, her husband was soon transferred to a new location. They did not know anyone there. Her husband began to associate with the wrong people at work. He was going to lunch with the guys. She soon sensed him pulling away. He started coming home later and later at night. Soon she found out he had joined a "men's club." She confronted him, and he soon filed for divorce.

It is important to recognize that we need to surround ourselves with positive influences. A good friend is priceless. The influence of immoral friends can destroy your life.

God, help me establish relationships that strengthen me to be more godly.

                                                    B. N.

> *. . . in all things showing yourself to be a pattern*
> *of good works; in doctrine showing integrity,*
> *reverence, incorruptibility, sound speech that*
> *cannot be condemned, that one who is an*
> *opponent may be ashamed, having nothing*
> *evil to say of you.*
> —TITUS 2:7–8

Many years ago I got a call to visit a very sick alcoholic at the local hospital. Dino was sprawled on the bed, his eyes sunken and glazed. A man about six feet tall, he weighed less than 120 pounds. He shook all the time. And he looked familiar.

Suddenly it came to me: He had called for help two years before. At that time he was athletic looking at about 180 very trim pounds, and he was arrogant about his drinking. In fact, he sipped a beer as we talked to him.

I reminded Dino of our earlier meeting. And he remembered me, wishing he had listened to us about getting help. When I assured him that it was still not too late, Dino said he intended to go to a treatment center when he left the hospital. We parted, saying we would keep in touch. I never heard from or saw him again.

God, thank You for reminding me how life could be for me if I do not stay close to You. I pray that all the Dinos in the world today might come to know You and Your healing love.

T. S.

*Let every man be swift to hear, slow to speak, slow
to wrath; for the wrath of man does not produce
the righteousness of God.*   —JAMES 1:19–20

Men have tremendous impact on their family members and others in their world. So it is important for men to remember the truth of these verses.

A woman called me and needed to talk about her husband. He had gone through financial hardships in his business. Lately, he had begun to yell at the children and at her without just cause. He would not listen to anything she had to say and his rage was getting more out of control each day. She had come to the point where she thought an intervention might be the only way to get through to him.

If we are not careful, we can lose control of how we express anger. We need God's guidance and direction when we feel angry. One way to gain better control is to be slow to speak. Think before you express your anger. Is it the right time, the right place? We need to be careful not to abuse others in rage.

God, help me to be quick to hear, slow to anger, and slow to speak.
                                                        B. N.

> *Do not be conformed to this world, but be*
> *transformed by the renewing of your mind,*
> *that you may prove what is that good and*
> *acceptable and perfect will of God.*
>
> —ROM. 12:2

Sometimes it is easy for us to see work as a race. We get up in the morning, put on our running shoes, and head to the racetrack, which is our job. The other runners are those who work beside us. We tend to believe that whoever gets the earliest start or runs the longest is the winner. This is an unusual race, though—it never ends. We run until we quit, get hurt, retire, or die.

Competition is good for any man to a point. But when it becomes harmful to himself and others, it has gone too far. When a man becomes too competitive at work, he loses his ability to be objective, and he is apt to make many mistakes. It is an impossibility to win the race, for there are no winners, only losers.

If you have a problem with being overly competitive at work, I suggest to you that your chances of succeeding are far greater if you run alone rather than running against someone else. Doing your own work, at your own pace, in your own way, will get you further in the long run. It may not appear that you are winning by earthly standards, but in eternity you may receive the checkered flag.

Lord, help me not to conform to the world's standards of success.

L. S.

Marriage is honorable among all, and the bed undefiled; but fornicators and adulterers God will judge.
—HEB. 13:4

Many men believe that it is "macho" to have slept with many women. To go out and conquer the "world of women" is a big deal in some men's eyes. On the other hand there are some men who are committed to marriage and slip up, becoming emotionally and often sexually involved with another woman.

Over and over I see the same scenario in couples who come for marriage counseling. Out of the blue, a wife finds out that her husband is involved with another woman. Quite commonly the man never made a conscious decision to cheat on his wife. He just enjoyed the business relationship with other women at work, and it grew more and more friendly. These affairs usually start out innocently, but often lead to destruction. They destroy the lives of everyone involved.

God commands us to keep the marriage bed pure—not just sexually pure, but emotionally pure as well. Don't even allow yourself to be involved in an emotional affair.

God, give me strength to keep my commitment to my wife strong and pure today.

> *And let us consider one another in order to stir up*
> *love and good works.*   —HEB. 10:24

The spirit of the twelfth step is to help one another to grow in God. And the Scripture asks us to do this by something we call consideration.

I take a negative outlook sometimes. In meetings people often get on my nerves. That's not to say that it's their problem because it's not! I'm the one with the bad attitude. And most often it shows itself in inconsiderateness.

The problem comes from my own exaggerated sense of entitlement. I think I have a right to treat others badly if I don't like them, but I don't.

What have I missed? Well, besides being rude and offending people, which is bad in itself, I have missed the chance to stir up love and good works in my brothers and sisters. I have lost the blessing of consideration for others.

God, help me to be more considerate and less judgmental. Grant me the blessing that comes from stirring up love and good works.

T. S.

I will praise You, for I am fearfully and
wonderfully made;
Marvelous are Your works,
And that my soul knows very well.
— PS. 139:14

Years ago I never had a good job. No matter how hard I tried, I never got anywhere. I had to walk to work while other men were driving. Almost every job I held paid right around minimum wage. For a time I never got along with my employers. Either I thought they treated me unfairly or I thought they didn't like me. I never got promotions or opportunities to move up, so I either quit or set myself up to be fired. I hated myself, my life, and my poverty, all of which I blamed on people that I believed didn't give me a fair chance.

Now that I am a doctor, I know that I was just living out an unconscious failure script. Unconsciously I hated myself and felt I deserved to fail in life. Once I discovered this truth, I was able to make headway. I learned to like myself and to accept God's unconditional love for me. I began to believe in myself and in turn believed that others could do likewise.

You may be able to relate to this story. If you have a strong urge to succeed but nothing ever seems to happen, then maybe you have a failure script.

What you don't know about yourself can hurt you

L. S.

> *Come to Me, all you who labor and are heavy
> laden, and I will give you rest. Take My yoke upon
> you and learn from Me, for I am gentle and lowly
> in heart, and you will find rest for your souls. For
> My yoke is easy and My burden is light.*
> —MATT. 11:28–30

While working through issues that relate to a man in recovery, we often feel burdened and overloaded. Grief, anger, bitterness, shame, and confusion are there. God encourages us to turn to Him for strength and refuge.

I remember one time in my life when I was under some strong emotional pressures. I was having trouble sleeping at night. I felt anxious most of the time. A friend came to me and shared these verses. He prayed for me and continued to encourage me. The Lord brought peace into my life, and I was able to work through the difficult time.

Often our being overburdened is of our own doing. We become overwhelmed because we are not following His plan for us. What might you be doing to cause you to feel so burdened?

God, help me to turn to You with the burdens of my life. May I find rest in You.

B. N.

He who loves silver will not be satisfied with silver;
Nor he who loves abundance, with increase.
This also is vanity.

—ECCL. 5:10

Money has a tight grip on many men today. They see their success tied up in the amount of money they make. They become slaves to obtaining more and more. What they have is never enough.

I know two men who have lost millions of dollars each. One reacted with despair and with anger that drove all his friends and family away from him. He could not face himself in the mirror because he no longer had even one million dollars in the bank. In his mind, money was who he was, rather than something he enjoyed. The other man found it difficult to face himself in the mirror, too. He didn't like losing the luxuries and privileges money had provided for him. But he adjusted and went on living. He and his wife worked together to live on their reduced income. He had enjoyed the money when he had it, but he found ways to live without it.

Solomon warns us that our happiness in life is not linked to how much we have or don't have. True happiness only comes in our relationship with God.

Lord, I pray I can see Your importance in my life and not be blinded by material possessions.

B. N.

Those who wait on the LORD
Shall renew their strength.
—IS. 40:28–31

As another year comes to a close you may be experiencing fatigue and a sense of burnout. The holidays can be a stressful time of facing family issues, as well as the issues related to recovery. It is important to remember that God is always there and that God does not become weary or tired.

Masculinity is closely associated with the image of strength. In the recovery process, you may not always feel very strong. God is always strong. In fact, He is strength itself, and He wants to give you His strength if you lean on Him.

As you think about this past year, how has your recovery been going? Are you feeling tired and weary? Have you wanted to give up? Stop right now and plan to spend some time waiting on God. God loves you and wants to strengthen you to make it through another year of the recovery process. Commit each day this next year to set aside some time to wait on the Lord.

Lord, as I wait on you, strengthen me with the power to face each day—one day at a time.

B. N.

About the Authors

Author of *Men Like Us* (Harold Shaw Publishers, 1990), Ted Scheuermann calls himself a professional layman. He is coordinator of MAN-TO-MAN, a program of the Christian Service Brigade, and is a recovering alcoholic with twelve years of sobriety. He has a ministry to the church through small groups and one-on-one discipleship and has written material for men's recovery groups, specifically those in Twelve Step programs.

Ted lives in Wheaton, Illinois.

Larry Stephens is a licensed professional counselor and a certified alcohol and drug abuse counselor in the state of Texas. Prior to joining the Minirth-Meier Clinic staff, he was a primary therapist for two treatment centers in Fort Worth, Texas. Stephens has a doctorate of education in psychology and counseling and a master of arts in marriage and family counseling from Southwestern Baptist Theological Seminary in Fort Worth, Texas.

Larry lives in the Dallas area.

Clinical director of Inpatient Services with the Minirth-Meier Clinic in Dallas, Brian Newman has a D.Phil. from Oxford Graduate School and a master of arts in counseling from Grace Theological Seminary in Winona Lake, Indiana. Brian is co-author of *Passages of Marriage* and *Love Is A Choice Workbook* and *Day by Day,* and lives with his wife and two children in Allen, Texas.

Bob Dyer is director of Seminars and Information Services for the Minirth-Meier Clinic in Dallas. A licensed minister, he has worked as an associate and counseling pastor in Tulsa, Oklahoma, and in Dallas. Dyer has a B.A. in psychology from Oklahoma Baptist University and a M.A. in Christian Education and Family Ministry from Dallas Theological Seminary.

Bob speaks to youth groups and men's groups and at family conferences on topics such as self-esteem, marriage, relationships, and youth conflicts and is a contributing writer for *Today's Better Life* magazine.

Bob lives with his wife and son in the Dallas area.